Better Homes and Gardens®

newclassicstyle

Better Homes and Gardens® Books
Des Moines, Iowa

contents

creating harmony

creating comfort

Better Homes and Gardens® Books
An imprint of Meredith® Books

New Classic Style
Editor: Vicki L. Ingham
Contributing Editors: Diane Carroll, Stephanie Davis, Claudia Franklin, Nancy Ingram, Stacy Kunstel, Joetta Moulden, Hilary Rose, Helen Thompson, Linda Baltzell Wright
Art Director: Mick Schnepf
Copy Chief: Terri Fredrickson
Copy and Production Editor: Victoria Forlini
Editorial Operations Manager: Karen Schirm
Managers, Book Production: Pam Kvitne, Marjorie J. Schenkelberg
Contributing Copy Editor: Jane Woychick
Contributing Proofreaders: Becky Etchen, Judy Friedman, Gretchen Kauffman, Nancy Ruhling

Contributing Photographers: King Au/Studio Au, Gordon Beall, Fran Brennan, Colleen Duffley, Tria Giovan, Ed Gohlich, Ken Gutmaker, Jenifer Jordan, Jocelyn Lee, Sylvia Martin, Janet Mesic-Mackie, William Stites
Indexer: Stephanie Reymann
Electronic Production Coordinator: Paula Forest
Editorial and Design Assistants: Kaye Chabot, Karen McFadden, Mary Lee Gavin

Meredith® Books
Editor in Chief: Linda Raglan Cunningham
Design Director: Matt Strelecki
Managing Editor: Gregory H. Kayko
Executive Editor, Home Decorating and Design: Denise L. Caringer

Publisher: James D. Blume
Executive Director, Marketing: Jeffrey Myers

creating
serenity

what goes with what

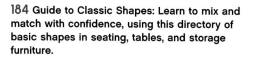

Executive Director, New Business Development: Todd M. Davis
Executive Director, Sales: Ken Zagor
Director, Operations: George A. Susral
Director, Production: Douglas M. Johnston
Business Director: Jim Leonard

Vice President and General Manager: Douglas J. Guendel

Better Homes and Gardens® Magazine
Editor in Chief: Karol DeWulf Nickell
Meredith Publishing Group
President, Publishing Group: Stephen M. Lacy
Vice President-Publishing Director: Bob Mate

Meredith Corporation
Chairman and Chief Executive Officer: William T. Kerr

Chairman of the Executive Committee: E. T. Meredith III
Copyright® 2003 by Meredith Corporation, Des Moines, Iowa.
First Edition.
All rights reserved. Printed in the United States of America.
Library of Congress Control Number: 2002109227
ISBN: 0-696-21403-2

All of us at Better Homes and Gardens® Books are dedicated to providing you with information and ideas to enhance your home. We welcome your comments and suggestions. Write to us at: Better Homes and Gardens Books, Home Decorating and Design Editorial Department, 1716 Locust St., Des Moines, IA 50309-3023.

If you would like to purchase any of our home decorating and design, cooking, crafts, gardening, or home improvement books, check wherever quality books are sold. Or visit us at: bhgbooks.com

Notes from a convert

I grew up with reproduction Duncan Phyfe mahogany furniture, and as a young adult, I considered Queen Anne antiques the epitome of beauty and grace. If I was conscious of modern furniture at all, I dismissed it as cheap, plastic, and impersonal. Then a few years ago, I saw a loft in which pieces by Heywood-Wakefield, Eames, and Bruno Mathsson were accented with 19th-century antiques and folk art. Suddenly I saw modern in a new light. Since then, the more I've looked at furniture created between the 1920s and the 1960s, the more I appreciate certain themes and forms—the organic, playful spirit of furniture designed by Scandinavians such as Finn Juhl and Alvar Aalto; the exquisitely graceful lines of the Cherner chair by Norman Cherner; and the clean, practical simplicity of cantilevered tubular-steel chairs by Marcel Breuer.

Although some of these designs are at least 50 years old, they continue to look current, fresh, even futuristic—and they continue to inspire designers. That enduring quality marks them as classics. Interior designers have long combined classic forms from the 18th and 19th centuries (and earlier), and they're now adding modern classics to the mix. Modern pieces loosen up a room full of traditional furniture, introducing cleaner lines and simplified shapes. Traditional pieces anchor a modern room and create a layered,

evolved feeling that blends comfortable familiarity with forward-looking excitement. In both cases, the eclectic blend embraces the present and future without abandoning the past.

This mix-and-match approach isn't new, of course. In both Europe and America, combining the most current furniture designs with older pieces has been a matter of necessity. Most people can't afford to throw out all their old furniture and start over—nor would they want to. As early as 1934, *Better Homes and Gardens®* magazine recognized that its readers wanted to freshen their rooms with the latest in home furnishings without giving up the pieces they loved. Interior Furnishings Director Christine Holbrook assured readers, "The best of today's furnishings will last, as do the best of the past, and in most instances the past agrees very well with the new."

In the pages that follow, you'll see examples of ways to achieve that blending of old and new. In each case, modern furnishings are the means to an end—and the end is a home that comforts and cheers you and expresses your special sense of style.

Vicki Ingham

Editor, *New Classic Style*

Coming to terms

What defines traditional versus modern style? And what is contemporary? Traditional style encompasses the decorative arts of western Europe, and by extension North America, from the 16th through the 19th century. Under that broad umbrella are many period and regional styles, each defined by characteristic kinds of ornamentation and decorative shapes; these developed as a result of local crafting traditions and furniture-making techniques as well as changes in taste. Fashions in furniture usually started at the top—with royalty—and filtered down. Historical or exotic influences, such as ancient Greek or Roman architecture or Egyptian and Chinese furniture forms and motifs, began to appear in European furniture design in the 18th century.

Modern furniture and decorative arts rejected ornament in favor of straightforward shapes that could be mass-produced. New industrial materials such as plywood and tubular steel were key, and designers created forms to reflect function and nothing more—no finials, no egg-and-dart molding, no carved flowers.

The roots of modern furniture design go back to the 1850s, when Prussian cabinetmaker Michael Thonet began bending rods of solid wood to make mass-produced furniture for cafes, restaurants, and hotels. His goal was to create lightweight, sturdy chairs that could be manufactured in large quantities. His most successful model, the Chair No. 14, appeared in his company catalog of 1859.

This chair and some of its variations inspired young architects working in the late 1920s. They liked its streamlined shape and the fact that its appearance reflected the requirements of material, machine manufacturing, and mass production rather than the whim of changeable fashion. That commitment to industrial methods and materials is a defining characteristic of progressive early-20th-century architecture and furniture design.

Movements in art and architecture are often named after the fact; the passage of time allows common themes to emerge. Magazines and catalogs showcasing the work of early avant-garde designers described it as either modern or contemporary. Since the 1960s, "modern" has come to mean a specific design philosophy anchored in a particular period of history spanning the late 1920s to the mid-1960s. "Contemporary" refers to whatever is being created at the present time in the latest style.

Which modern?

Modern furniture actually represents several stages and sources of development. The first stage (and source) occurred in the 1920s in Germany, where the Bauhaus school was the center of experimentation and creative activity. Work at the Bauhaus contributed to a revolutionary approach to architecture, the International style, which used steel-reinforced concrete to construct buildings with skins of glass and free-flowing interiors. The school also became the source of radically new furniture design, thanks in large part to Marcel Breuer. Inspired by the bent-steel handlebars on his new bicycle, Breuer began experimenting with tubular steel as a material for furniture. In 1925, he produced an armchair for artist and fellow teacher Wassily Kandinsky, using tubular steel for the frame and fabric panels for the seat, back, and sides. Although Breuer continued to adjust and improve the design until late 1927 or early 1928, the original design encouraged others in Europe and America to experiment further with tubular steel for chairs, tables, stools, and sofas. Tubular steel became the quintessential modern material, touted as lightweight, inexpensive, durable, and hygienic.

The Nazis rejected modernism, and by the late 1930s, the school's leading members had left Germany. Many ended up in the United States where, as teachers, artists, and architects, they disseminated their rigorous and dogmatic vision of modernism.

Americans had already been introduced to modernism, however, through the work of industrial designers such as Donald Deskey, Gilbert Rohde, Norman Bel Geddes, Russel Wright, and Raymond Loewy. Donald Deskey, for example, had seen firsthand the work of French designers in Paris at the 1925 L'Exposition Internationale des Arts Decoratifs et Industriels Modernes (from which comes the name Art Deco). He sketched interiors, furniture, and decorative objects that he saw there and probably visited the Bauhaus too. In 1927, Deskey began using tubular steel and mass-production processes to produce furniture and lighting.

Unlike the doctrinaire adherents of Bauhaus modernism, American designers weren't bound by a set of theories, so they had no compunction about combining the decorative effects of exotic veneers (in the manner of Art Deco) with plain, straight-lined geometric forms or controlled, streamlined curves. They were, however, committed to using industrial materials and technology—cadmium-plated tubular steel, brushed nickel, Bakelite, glass, synthetic fibers—and to mass production of objects shorn of decorative ornament. Even the traditional material of wood could be used to express the modern style: Gilbert Rohde and Russel Wright each designed collections of maple and birch furniture for Heywood-Wakefield in the 1930s, using sweeping, aerodynamic lines similar to those that were applied to everything from vacuum cleaners to refrigerators during the Depression. Americans were in love with speed, and lines and shapes that expressed the theme

of movement, whether by airplane, car, or train, captured the very essence of modernity.

In the late 1930s, Scandinavian architects such as Bruno Mathsson and Alvar Aalto also took the modernist ideas of mass production, functionalism, and elimination of ornament and applied them to wood. Using blond birch plywood and heat-molding techniques, they produced graceful, organic furniture that was modern in concept and appearance, yet more approachable than the German tubular steel (which was criticized at the time for being clinical and mechanistic).

World War II stalled most furniture innovation and production, but after the war, modern design revived with fresh energy. A new generation of architects and industrial designers continued experiments with molded plywood and began working with molded plastic, laminates, aluminum, and stainless steel. The goods produced during this period, from the mid-1940s to the late 1950s, have become known among collectors as midcentury modern.

Modern revival

Tastes and fashions change, and by the late 1960s many Americans had begun to shed their modern interiors in favor of American country, Victorian Revival, or English-country cottage styles. Now, after 20 or 30 years of cozy clutter, the desire for cleaner, simpler, less fussy interiors is returning, and icons of modernism are in demand as the perfect tools to achieve that look. The distilled purity of Bauhaus modernism, the organic warmth of Scandinavian style, and the spirited inventiveness of American design offset the carving and curlicues of antiques. Combining the modern and the antique (or reproductions of antiques) creates a look that's comfortably eclectic yet visually exciting.

There's no one recipe for mixing modern and traditional classics. Let one style dominate and accent it with the other, or mix half and half, depending on what you already own and what you love. The goal is to create interiors that express who you are and suit the way you live. To ensure a successful blend, look for relationships between shapes and scale and unify with color.

In the pages that follow, you will see how 14 homeowners have used shape and color to mix and match classic furnishings. For more help on creating combinations, turn to the "Guide to Classic Shapes" on page 184. To learn more about the designers who have created the furnishings we use, review the biographical sketches at the back of the book. Finally, for sources of new and vintage modern furnishings and accessories, see the Resources section beginning on page 208.

creating

harmony

Harmony results from matching curve to curve,
straight line to straight line, **repeating shapes** to create unity,
inserting contrast to invite **variety**.

Dr. Robert and Elinor Turkel
Tampa, Florida

"I realized that all modern bored me and so did all traditional. What was exciting was the mix.

joy in the mix

It was 1967. Modernism was well-established as the accepted style for forward-thinking architects, interior designers, and consumers. When newlyweds Dr. Robert and Elinor Turkel began furnishing their first home in Tampa, Florida, Elinor recalls, "We started with Knoll and Eames, icons of modernism. The Barcelona table was the first piece we bought for our apartment."

Above: A 1960s painting that Elinor Turkel picked up at an antiques store hangs over a stainless-steel table in the entry; the muted tones and geometric shapes appeal to her modernist sensibilities. A coconut-wood lamp sheds welcoming light on a pair of small vases by contemporary Venetian glass designer Carlo Moretti.

Left: The golden patina of antique Hepplewhite chairs contrasts with the white metal finish of a pedestal table designed by architect Eero Saarinen in 1956, but the chairs' straight lines correspond to the table's cool, sleek shape.

Below: The townhouse exterior has the charm of a Key West cottage, with clapboard siding, gabled roof and dormer, columns, deep moldings, and shutters.

"We bought very few things, but everything was good," Elinor continues. After almost 10 years of collecting in what Elinor calls her "Lucite period," she hired a designer to help her finish the job. "When it was done, I sat down and cried," she recalls. "It was a horrible environment, everything hard and cold. For about five years, I vacuumed my living room and never looked at it."

Then one day while her husband was at work, she hired a truck to cart away everything in the living room, except the sectional sofa and the Barcelona table. "I sold almost everything and redid the living room and dining room in traditional antiques," she says, laughing. That marked the beginning of what she calls her formal period. On the advice of another interior designer, Elinor banished to storage the few modern pieces she had kept. Then she filled her house with 18th- and 19th-century pieces and flowery fabrics. "In the 1980s, everybody was doing chintz," says Elinor. "It was all very froufrou, 400 things on every table."

Little by little, however, the midcentury pieces began to creep back in. "I missed them," Elinor says. She realized that an all-modern house bored her, but so did one decorated in an entirely traditional style. "What was exciting was the mix," she says. "So I kept the antiques I absolutely loved, sold the ones I didn't, and started mixing in tag-sale finds with what I had." Now, she says, "It's me. It feels like home for the first time."

Above: A wall-mounted zebrawood credenza by Tampa interior designer Leo Mark Hampton coordinates with the mantel in the adjacent living room (see page 16). Teamed with a painting by Palm Beach artist Billie Hightower, the credenza introduces a sleek contemporary element into a setting dominated by traditional shapes.

Opposite: In the dining room, 20th-century Italian reproductions of Louis XVI chairs covered in fuchsia silk draw up to a square dining table that the Turkels commissioned from a local craftsman. The beveled-glass top rests on a walnut base inspired by English library tables. The Chinese altar table, carved from elm, is one of Elinor's favorite antique pieces. It serves as a sideboard, holding two antique Chinese majolica temple jars that have been converted to lamps; the tiny Foo dogs, dating from the 13th century, add a dash of bold color. Dove gray walls and red oak floors throughout the first floor make a warm but quiet backdrop for the couple's wide-ranging collection of furnishings and art.

Contrasting and repeating shapes

The repeating curves on the table pedestal continue the rolling movement of the acrylic bench (far right) and other rounded shapes; the boxy upholstered chair from contemporary furniture designer Thomas O'Brien provides a balancing visual pause. Its orderly geometry, along with that of the Chinese cabinet and the coffee table (opposite), offers a counterpoint to all the curves to give the room a feeling of stability and solidity.

Assertive curves

The C curves of an acrylic bench, probably made in the early 1970s, repeat the curving rhythms of the Platner stool (below), the Chippendale bench legs (see page 17), the rolled-arm sofa, and the pedestal side table (left). The repeating shapes set up a harmonious flow through the room. Elinor found the bench in a thrift store and had the seat re-covered in beige imitation cloth suede.

This journey to find her true style has taken place over 35 years of marriage, during which Robert has been content to let his wife's passion for decorating shape their home. His preferences are for the spare simplicity of Japanese art and design, so their current mix of modern with traditional is more to his liking than the excesses of the 1980s. Still, says Elinor, "He will tell you he thinks I have a few too many things for him. He likes one thing on each surface."

If the clean lines of modern furniture suit Robert's sensibilities, the individuality of the pieces attracts Elinor. "The modern things were designed in the 1920s and 1930s and still looked contemporary in the 1970s and even today," she says. The antiques also offer uniqueness, with qualities of beauty and craftsmanship that

Opposite: A room with 14-foot ceilings calls for a commanding piece of furniture to suit the scale of the space. A 17th-century Chinese kitchen cupboard answers the purpose, offering storage for the television and books. Beside a boxy upholstered chair stands a modern table; its shaped pedestal recalls the stools designed by Charles and Ray Eames in 1960 for the Time-Life offices and repeats in multiples the clean, curving shape of the Platner wire stool. The painting beside the Chinese cupboard was commissioned several years ago from a local artist, Laurie Ramirez; the colors find a happy echo in the silk pillow on the sofa. Behind the sofa, Chinese figurines from the 1930s, made into lamps, and a pair of Foo dogs add a global note to the decorating scheme. Oriental porcelain always has been a staple for formal traditional interiors, but it works equally well with modern furniture.

Glass and steel

Designed by architect Ludwig Mies van der Rohe in 1930 for furniture manufacturer Knoll International, the Barcelona coffee table has become a classic. Heavy ¾-inch-thick polished glass appears to float on a stainless-steel base, providing an elegant surface for cocktails or books without adding visual clutter to a room. Elinor keeps the look from being cold and hard by grounding the table on a new flokati rug. The Greek wool rugs, hip in the 1960s and 1970s, evoke a retro look but also suit a more eclectic style.

Industrial metal

Although crafted from modern industrial materials—nickel-plated steel with fabric over foam—this stool designed by Warren Platner in 1966 harbors organic inspiration. Its shape recalls that of a mushroom or a sheaf of wheat, streamlined and simplified. Platner wanted to evoke "the kind of decorative, gentle, graceful... design that appeared in a period style like Louis XV" but to achieve the effect through rational construction rather than applied ornament.

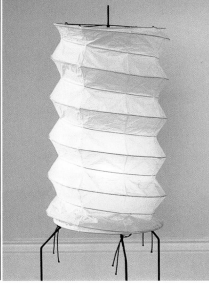

Chippendale shapes

With its knee-shape cabriole legs and ball-and-claw feet, this 18th-century Chippendale bench seems ready to start scampering around the room. "Cabriole" is from the French "to caper," and Thomas Chippendale clearly had frolicking animals in mind when he developed the design, which was applied to legs for chairs, tables, and secretaries. The form finds a distant echo in the metal base of the Akari light (right) that stands behind the bench.

Light sculpture

Inspired by the paper lanterns used for night fishing in Japan, Japanese-American sculptor Isamu Noguchi designed a variety of lamps in the 1950s using mulberry paper, bamboo strips, and an internal metal support. He named them "Akari," which means illumination. Possessing distinctive sculptural form, Noguchi's paper constructions also sculpt space with ambient light.

she finds irresistible. To blend pieces of various periods and styles, she looks for repeating or complementary shapes and harmonies of form, so the resulting combinations ease the eye around the room. The neutral palette, anchored with chocolate brown and enlivened with doses of fuchsia and pea green, also knits together shapes from different centuries and design traditions.

Blending Styles

One of the keys to the successful mix is scale, Elinor says. Individual pieces are in scale with each other and with the rooms they occupy. The upholstered and rattan chairs in the living room, for example, are identical in scale, even though their shapes and materials are quite different. Both are balanced by the shape and size of the sofa, whose curved arms and clean lines communicate unfussy comfort. The Chinese cupboard, a 17th-century piece that serves as an entertainment center, is tall enough to command attention in the lofty space, and its warm nut-brown finish provides a visual anchor in the mostly neutral scheme. Tobacco brown silk draperies framing the front window fall in soft columns of color that emphasize the architectural drama.

Another reason that the Turkels' mix works so well is that most of the furniture and accessories, whether antique or modern, have streamlined, simple lines and shapes. "Nothing is too ornate or heavily carved," says Elinor.

Opposite: A meeting of icons: A Chippendale bench and a Warren Platner wire stool (designed in 1966) face off over the Barcelona coffee table, which was designed in 1930 by architect Ludwig Mies van der Rohe. Over the zebrawood mantel hangs a painting by Billie Hightower, a prominent Palm Beach-based artist, now deceased. His modernist treatment of a traditional figural subject captures the creative tension Elinor seeks to achieve in her decorating. On the mantel shelf, Carlo Moretti vases repeat colors found elsewhere in the room, and the wood sculpture—coated in cobalt blue pastel pigment—adds powerful complementary punch. In the corner, an abstract garden sculpture balances the tall Chinese cupboard on the opposite wall.

> " I got bored with all the modern and wanted something new, fresh, different. **So I sold everything except for a few pieces—I'm sick about it now; I shouldn't have done it all at once, but who knew?** "

The exceptions are found in the dining room. "That's the one place I allowed myself to keep the froufrou," she admits. "I decided to keep the Victorian candlesticks and see how they worked. Once I put them on the table, they never left." It's not surprising that the pair of gilt and crystal candlesticks found a home so readily; kindred spirits surround them—an ornate mirror frame, shapely crystals that drip like fat raindrops from wall sconces and the chandelier, and the black and gold-painted dining chairs, which are 20th-century Italian reproductions of Louis XVI side chairs. For a side table, the Turkels purchased an antique Chinese altar table made of elm. Long and narrow, it fit the space perfectly and has become one of Elinor's favorite antiques. On the adjacent wall, a zebrawood buffet recalls mid-20th-century modern wall-mounted credenzas, but is a new piece by local interior designer Leo Mark Hampton. The dining table is itself a fusion of old and new styles.

Right: The interplay of shapes and colors produces an invigorating mix in the breakfast room. The color of the parsons-style buffet table echoes the warm tones of the antique Hepplewhite chairs and the hardwood floors, and the no-nonsense geometry of the buffet resonates with the straight chair legs. Against these rigid verticals, the stem of the metal table blossoms upward, its white skin mirroring the room's trim color.

The Eero Saarinen pedestal table was the couple's first kitchen table. "It had the pedestal chairs around it originally, but those got thrown out," Elinor says with chagrin. Now she teams this midcentury modern icon with 18th-century Hepplewhite chairs in the harlequin style, so called because the splats vary. A George Kovacs lamp illuminates the table from overhead. Above the sideboard, another Billie Hightower painting warms the breakast room wall with color.

Commissioned from a local woodworker, it features column-style walnut legs modeled on those of English library tables and is topped with ¾-inch beveled glass.

Architectural**Mix**

The architecture of the townhouse expresses a similar marriage of traditional and modern. Clapboard siding, gabled roof, columns, deep moldings, and shutters stamp the exterior with the charm of a Key West cottage. Inside, the Turkels opted to eliminate crown moldings, pillars, and a big mantel with fluted woodwork—all called for in the original plans. They kept only the molded baseboards and windowsills and the muntins dividing the large windows. Instead of the large, ornate fireplace, they chose a sleek slate hearth and surround, and had Leo Mark Hampton create a spare zebrawood mantel topped with a glass shelf.

The artful and restrained blending of styles captivates Elinor: *"Harmony means peaceful and balanced to me, and that's how my home feels. I can't believe how lucky I am when I look at these rooms and think how beautiful the light is coming in here, and how wonderful this object or that piece looks with the light falling on it, how glorious and joyful it all is."*

Left and opposite: The dark finish of the clean-lined contemporary furniture anchors the all-white bedroom. Curvaceous French bergères introduce softening lines and repeat the black and chocolate notes. Fern prints hung in tidy grids add refreshing, soft color.

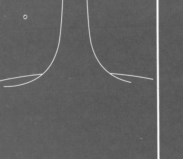

Benjamin Noriega-Ortiz (seated) and Steven Wine. Manhattan, New York

I use color and shape to take midcentury modern to the next level.

comping with shapes

"I've always mixed across style periods," says Benjamin Noriega-Ortiz. Pieces from the 1950s, 1960s, and 1970s can make a room of traditional furnishings look cleaner and younger. But Benjamin's overriding interest has little to do with the pedigree of furnishings and everything to do with shape and color.

Above: Benjamin Noriega-Ortiz designed a clear acrylic peninsula to divide the kitchen (behind the curtain) from the living area. The peninsula is "there but not there," enhancing the sense of space. Acrylic furniture was popular in the 1960s, and Benjamin sees it making a return. "As long as you don't copy anything old," he says, "it still looks new."

Left: The plaster lamp base, dating from the 1940s, has an exuberant, Baroque quality that reminds Benjamin of Fred Astaire movies and Florida.

"I use color and shape to take midcentury modern to the next level," he says. The shape of a piece is a given, so color becomes a tool for exaggerating or emphasizing it. Color also provides the means to marry disparate pieces and create a cohesive whole.

"If you select a color," says Benjamin, "you should go all out through the whole place with it." Color used in abundance makes the space sculptural and more modern, he adds. When he redecorated his Manhattan apartment three years ago, he used metallic aluminum paint to cover all walls and ceilings except those in the bedrooms, which are flat white. ("Bedrooms should be calmer and more serene," he says. "You can go for drama in the public areas.") Because the corner apartment's two exterior walls are mostly glass, daylight illuminates the 44th-floor space from morning until night. In the morning, the light in the living room is silvery, but in the afternoon, it turns warm and golden.

Light&Space

The changing light quality results largely from the reflective paint treatment. All of the furniture went into storage, and Benjamin and his partner, Steven Wine, had to move out while professional painters went to work, spraying walls and ceilings with industrial-quality aluminum paint and a fixative. The process required 10 coats applied over a period of three days. "It took forever to dry," says Benjamin.

The aluminum color provides a luminous backdrop for furnishings and floor coverings in shades of buttermilk, snow, vanilla, and smoke. Glass and acrylic pieces virtually disappear, so the white and silver scheme is serene and space-expanding. A mirrored wall further enlarges the sense of space, reflecting views and emphasizing the light. The white wall-to-wall carpet is a first for Benjamin, who usually chooses wood or marble for flooring. The warm texture invites visitors to take off their shoes and sit on the floor. "This carpet also has a calming quality because it looks like raked sand," he adds.

Opposite: Benjamin has lived in this Manhattan apartment since 1988 and gave it this shimmering facelift in 1999. The main living area accommodates conversation and dining. The pedestal dining table and chairs can be pulled into the room when there are four for dinner. Benjamin's partner, Steven Wine, found the chrome and glass coffee table as a castoff. Austrian shades made of a synthetic thermal fabric from Jack Lenore Larsen dress the windows. The sliding glass doors and windows on the right wall overlook the Hudson River; the far wall of windows frames a view once dominated by the World Trade Center.

An African drum serves as a side table for the Eero Saarinen Womb chair. Benjamin uses ethnic art as well as natural materials, such as feathers and fur (an influence drawn from fashion), to introduce texture into a clean-lined room.

Opposite: A friend found Casper the Friendly Ghost at a flea market, and Benjamin liked its kitschy quality. The stacked aluminum table is a remake of a 1932 design. Its curves soften the corner of the boxy room.

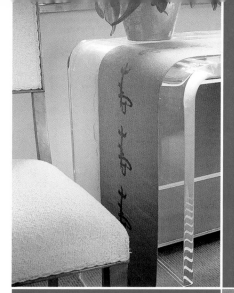

Curve meets curve

The sweeping line of the molded acrylic chair resonates with the shapely curve of the Biedermeier table pedestal (right). The round top and concave base of the table also play off the lines of the chair. Related colors help unify the pieces.

Versatile acrylic

Clear acrylic pieces (above) mix easily with traditional wood furniture because the acrylic almost disappears. This nearly invisible, clean-lined desk doesn't compete for attention with the Biedermeier chair, and rounded corners keep the look friendly.

Transitional shapes

A Chinese altar table, stripped of its finish and topped with white acrylic, serves as a bedside table (left). Below it, the telephone rests on a tray. The curving shape of the table apron echoes the profiles of French and English antiques, blending this style of furniture with traditional pieces. The absence of ornament—no high-relief carving on the apron or legs—makes the piece compatible with modern furniture as well.

Opposite: Benjamin painted the Biedermeier table silver to emphasize its bold sculptural shape. Pocket-size mirrors attached to clear monofilament form a glittering, light-reflecting curtain at the end of the banquette. The mirrors visually separate the living area from the hall to the bedrooms.

Color&Shape

"I look at every material as a color," Benjamin says. "Wood is a color, as is fabric, so if I want to exaggerate a shape, I 'eliminate' the wood with paint so you focus on the shape." The sofa is a case in point. Dating from the 1930s, it brings a hint of Hollywood glamour to the apartment. Benjamin painted the wooden legs and frame buttermilk to blend with the linen velvet upholstery, so the eye takes in the piece as a sculptural whole. Even more daring (purists might say cavalier) was his treatment of an antique Biedermeier pedestal table. He had it cut down to a more comfortable height for dining and then had it coated with aluminum paint to match the walls and ceiling of the apartment. "It wasn't a fine antique," he notes, although he acknowledges that Biedermeier enthusiasts might be horrified. The result, however, is to take attention away from the table's pedigree and to focus instead on the bold mass and classic lines of the pedestal and base. The table becomes a postmodern statement, a freewheeling

interplay between classical shape and contemporary industrial color and texture. Freed from antique associations, the curves of the pedestal echo the sweeping lines of smoky acrylic Steen Ostergaard chairs from the 1970s. "Because the living room is a box, all the furniture has curves," notes Benjamin. "Everything is rounded and curved and slightly skewed in its placement."

Art&Architecture

Benjamin earned a master's degree in architecture at the University of Puerto Rico, then earned a master's in architecture and urban design from Columbia University in New York. His training in Puerto Rico was much more aesthetically oriented than most U.S. architecture degrees. "It involved studying art, ceramics, painting, photography," he says, "so you hang out with artists and you are looking at interiors as art."

Taking the required two years of art photography taught him to see rooms in a photographic way as well. He composes spaces as if for the camera in the sense that he considers how people will approach the room, and he identifies the natural center of interest. He then designs so that the first impression makes the most impact. In the living room of his apartment, the first thing visitors see is the sofa, curled like a cat in the sun. The dining table and Womb chair act as a frame, directing attention toward a stunning view of downtown Manhattan. This way of working with space is fundamental to Benjamin's blending of modern and classical aesthetics: Arranging furniture around a focal point is a classical approach; creating the feeling of openness is a modern idea. "When you leave the room, I give you something to look at too,"

Opposite top: Originally designated the No. 70, the upholstered tubular-steel chair designed by Eero Saarinen in 1947–1948 became known as the Womb chair because its size and shape invited curling up. The chair and ottoman have been reissued by Knoll International. In the background, the entry hall gives departing guests a last view of the living room.
Opposite bottom: A Roman urn dating from 300 B.C.E. introduces a classical profile; flowers add color while clear glass vases disappear into the background; a stacked-rock sculpture adds warm natural texture; Isamu Noguchi's Chicken lamp illuminates the banquette.

he adds. In his apartment, guests see a reflection of the living room in the mirrored entry hall as they head toward the door.

Antique&Modern

Contrasts between antique and modern are evident throughout the apartment: A wall-mounted CD player is juxtaposed with an old-fashioned (working) rotary telephone; traditional Austrian shades are fashioned from a synthetic thermal material; flat-screen televisions and computer printers rest on antique tables or old boxes covered in vellum; and a vintage lamp illuminates the laptop computer on the clear acrylic desk in the bedroom. Benjamin

The pedestal chair is Philippe Starck's interpretation of the 1957 Champagne chair. A working rotary telephone sits on a Chinese ceramic table below a wall-mounted CD player and radio. The sliding door leads to a balcony overlooking the Hudson River.

Below: A corner of the bedroom serves as a home office. The see-through quality of the desk, a molded clear acrylic table designed by Benjamin, keeps the room from feeling cluttered. The Biedermeier chairs wear their original finish; Benjamin upholstered the backs to blend with the wood and the fronts and seats to blend with the walls. A vintage Apollo Electronic Company lamp sheds light on the work surface. The horse sculpture on the windowsill is by a Puerto Rican sculptor and has been with Benjamin since he was 20.

Above: A white-on-white scheme in the bedroom induces a feeling of serenity, and wood elements add warmth. Embroidered organza veils the bed with luxurious texture. The upholstered headboard stretches from wall to wall, subtly adding depth to the room. An original Gio Ponti mirror hangs above the bed to reflect light. Ponti, founder of the influential design magazine *Domus*, was a proponent of mixing old and new and believed that modernism—form follows function—could be compatible with decoration and ornament.

embraces technology as part of the furniture but combines it with the patina of old wood, ancient marble, and ethnic art to create a richly textured environment that feels serene and inviting.

The guest bedroom has a more consistently 1950s look (see pages 34–35), thanks to the style-setting impact of two mid-1950s dressers, a Gilbert Rohde lamp, and a collection of funky tripod lamps picked up on eBay. Even in this room, however, old and new mix. The chenillelike bedspread is a Moroccan wedding blanket (hundreds of metal disks stitched among the tufted threads jingle to signal that the marriage has been consummated). On the dresser, a flat-screen television forms part of an eclectic still life with a vintage fan, 1950s lamps, and a painting by an early-20th-century Puerto Rican artist. The scene depicted, part of the chapel of San Cristobal, is one that Benjamin knew well when he was a child in Puerto Rico.

"Growing up in Puerto Rico has a lot to do with my interiors," says Benjamin. "They're light and airy and open as a result of my living in a warm climate. Also, I was around water all the time, so living here beside the river is great for me." The philosophical influence of water on his approach to design becomes apparent too. "There is a lot of fluidity in my interiors, things flowing from one room to another," he says.

Opposite: Feather-covered lamps appear to float languorously over the bedside tables. The lamps are the creation of Steven Wine's company, And Bob's Your Uncle, which produces custom-designed lighting and accessories. Monofilament suspends the lamp from the ceiling; the wiring is concealed in plastic tubing that coils on the tabletop.

Life&Art

Benjamin's affinity for midcentury modern furniture isn't surprising, because he grew up with that style. "When I was 6 or 7, my parents had Danish Modern, which was perfect for the climate," he says. The thin lines looked light and airy, and the foam was lighter and cooler to sit on than traditional down filling. "When I was a teenager," he says, "they went traditional."

Benjamin didn't follow their stylistic about-face. He did, however, absorb a classical approach to interior design by working with renowned designer John Saladino. After nine years with the company, Benjamin opened his own office. His work has been featured in most of the top interior design magazines, and *House Beautiful* named him one of 101 "Today's Stylemakers Designers."

His portfolio of residences that have appeared in magazines shows exquisite interiors that are clean and serene—but each is different, representing a custom solution for the client and site. As his own client, Benjamin has free rein to play with shapes. The result is a fresh eclecticism that lifts his apartment to the level of art—a three-dimensional sculpture he can live in.

Above left: The combination lamp and bedside table is one of many innovative, dual-purpose products that industrial designer Gilbert Rohde developed for furniture manufacturer Herman Miller in the 1930s, moving that company into the forefront of modern design.

Left: A collection of 1950s lamps along the windowsill exemplifies another trend of midcentury modernism, a fanciful exuberance that could cross into kitsch.

Opposite: A Moroccan wedding blanket covers the bed with texture that resembles chenille. Light glints off the metal disks sewn onto the fabric—they jingle when the blanket moves. The still life arranged on the two 1950s dressers repeats in microcosm Benjamin's mix of periods and styles. The 1950s lamps frame a vintage fan, a flat-screen TV, and an early-20th-century painting of the chapel of San Cristobal in Puerto Rico.

Ronn and Pat Ives
Virginia Beach,
Virginia

"Good, useful design and art *always* express their time and place. There is no such thing as timeless!

object lessons

"**I think the 20th** century was one of the most interesting, creative, and frightening centuries of all time," says artist and antiques dealer Ronn Ives. Because art and design are tangible, powerful expressions of a culture at a given moment in time, he's fascinated by 20th-century design in all of its manifestations, from art and architecture to furniture and flatware.

Above: In the entry hall, a signed Alfredo Barbini glass lamp sits on an oak and aluminum cabinet beneath a metal wall sculpture. As a collector, Ronn Ives looks for signed pieces because they will appreciate in value, but even unsigned pieces, if well-designed, are a good investment.

Below: Contemporary houses of the late 1950s and early 1960s typically have asymmetrical shapes and rooflines and a gridlike arrangement of solids and voids (walls and windows). Ronn chose a historically correct aqua for the cladding and window trim, both for authenticity and because he wanted the color to work well with the sky, the landscape, and changes in light according to the weather.

Opposite: Rhythmic curves keep the eye moving around the living room. Straight lines and strong verticals, such as the handmade Paul Evans iron table lamp, keep the curves in bounds. Bare wood floors add warm color while enhancing the feeling of openness. The Paul McCobb cabinet holds the television and other electronic equipment. Roman shades made from vintage fabric unfold to cover the windows at night.

Right and below: An original and rare Eames dining set defines the dining area. The bold green in the Owen McHugh nonobjective painting is echoed in the collection of green vases and bottles on top of the Paul McCobb dining room cabinet and hutch near the door.

That passion for a particular period rules out an anything-goes eclecticism; at the same time, the house doesn't look like a 1958 stage set either. Instead, Ronn aims for a certain authenticity, with furnishings that relate to the architecture and to each other in terms of design. You won't find any souvenirs from the 18th century here, but you will find an artful mixing across the decades of the last century, with meticulously composed arrangements of furniture and objects creating a harmonious, comfortable interior.

StyleShift

When Ronn and his wife, Pat, moved into their suburban split-level in Virginia Beach, Virginia, their furniture consisted primarily of Ronn's American Machine Age/Art Deco collection. In the open, light-filled spaces, however, the low, dark furnishings from the 1930s and 1940s looked wrong. So he began selling pieces, replacing them with modern classics that would better "cooperate and 'converse' with the building," he says.

Like much suburban architecture of the late 1950s, the house has an open floor plan in the public or social spaces; the ceilings soar to 18 feet in some areas, and the staircase connecting the three levels is almost entirely open. Morning light pours into the living room through the grid of windows that forms one wall.

Harmonic**Shapes**

In keeping with the abundance of natural light, Ronn says, "I wanted most of the masses to float, to be lighter in tone and warmer in color than what I'd had before; however, I wanted the sofa, which has none of those characteristics, to be the anchor of the room." An Oscar de la Renta design produced in the 1940s, the sofa is stuffed with goose down and covered with velour, and it's perfect for sleeping or watching movies. Although it is visually hefty, the sofa finds an answering curve in the biomorphic Noguchi coffee table, the smiling lines of Slice chairs designed by Pierre Paulin, and the four-leaf-clover shape of a glass-and-oak Modern Age side table. The curves set up a feeling of rhythmic movement that pauses to meet counterbalancing rectangles and verticals—the Paul McCobb cabinet, the Paul Evans iron lamp, wall art, and pieces from Ronn's glass and ceramic collections.

Color comes into play too. "For many of the spaces in the house, I want deep cool colors and warm neutrals to dominate," he says. "I intentionally juxtapose them with the complementary colors of the wooden floors, the wooden furniture, and some of the art and glass. I want a restful feeling, but not sleepy." The rooms are as much an expression of his artistry as the drawings and prints he used to create, and he says, "I get to walk through this project."

Furnishing most of the home's interior is Ronn's job. Pat, a kitchen and bath designer, is interested in the interiors too, but puts most of her creative energies into the garden and yard.

Opposite: The furniture is functional and comfortable, but that doesn't preclude a sculptural arrangement. A George Nelson end table and an Eero Saarinen side chair form a still life beneath the Owen McHugh painting that marks the transition from living area to dining area. The floor lamp, designed by Gerald Thurston for Lightolier, reverses the upswept curves of an Italian bowl by Guido Gambone. An African mask on the wall recalls the inspiration early modernist painters found in African art.

Right: A second Owen McHugh painting and McCobb cabinet fill the wall behind the sofa. This spare display, with plenty of space around each item, shows off the shape of each object and creates a quiet effect. Repeating colors unify the display: A working "Ericofon" telephone by Ericsson balances a handthrown bud vase by Carolyn Klug, and the orange tone of a signed ceramic ashtray by Marcello Fantoni echoes the hue of the bulbous Italian glass bud vase by Flavio Poli.

Collector Class

Prolific ceramic and glass production in the 20th century poured an abundance of functional and decorative items into the market. Here are a few of Ronn's treasures.

1. A silverplate and enamel bowl designed by Alexander Calder in the late 1950s combines sleek shape and a jolt of color.

2. From left, an Italian ceramic vase for Raymor, a ceramic vase for Poole, and a Marcello Fantoni 13-inch bottle-form vase for Raymor feature matte, high-gloss, and textured dripped glazes, respectively.

3. Handmade Italian ceramic lighter and cigarette box for Raymor document an era when smoking was chic and widespread.

4. A three-color handblown glass vase made in 1981 by Michael David and Kit Karbler stands behind a long, low 1950s glass vase by Erickson.

5. A handblown aqua and cobalt-cased Italian glass bowl produced in the 1950s feels as weighty as it looks.

6. A 1950s Italian ceramic pitcher with a majolica glaze combines a centuries-old technique with modern graphic design.

7. A striped Glidden Parker and Fong Chow vase made for Raymor in the 1950s forms part of a green-themed display. Diffferent shapes add interest.

8. A still life of varied shapes brings the eye from back to front and left to right. A stylized animal decorates the signed white and black ceramic vase by Ron Scharf; a red and white-cased glass bottle form by Otto Brauer (late 1960s), a signed ceramic "corsage" vase by Russel Wright for Bauer, and a ceramic ashtray by Ingrid Atterburg for Upsala-Ekeby, about 1955, lead the eye back to a large red, orange, and black Italian ceramic vase for Raymor.

Opposite: A screen print by Richard Anuszkiewicz, 1969, complements the collection of green and blue ceramics and glass on the hutch. Another Gerald Thurston floor lamp, with a green-gray shade, illuminates the dining area. Ronn experiments constantly with lighting. "I would rather use 10 lamps with 15 watts each than just one with 150 watts," he says. He prefers warm light aimed in a "spot" fashion, he says, to sculpt space.

Right: After World War II, "burst" patterns inspired by fascination with atomic power appeared on a wide variety of products, including Franciscan Starburst dishware.

Below: The design on Federal Fantasy glassware from 1957 recalls the shape of Isamu Noguchi's glass-top coffee table, a "blob" or "amoeba" form that appeared as a reaction to the rational, geometric designs of the 1920s and early 1930s.

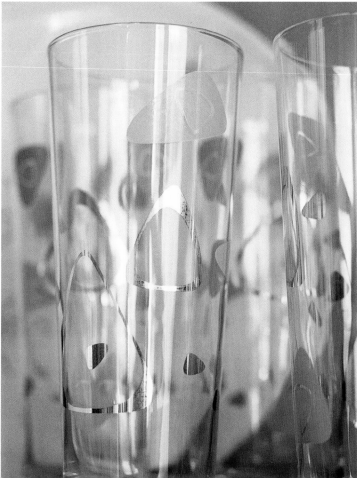

Collection**Addiction**

As the owner of FUTURES Antiques, which specializes in vintage modern design, Ronn constantly searches for original pieces that have "soul" as well as investment potential. Inevitably, some of his finds come home, sometimes to visit, sometimes to stay. "I have a policy," says Ronn. "If I bring a new acquisition into our home collection, an old one must leave for FUTURES." A set of 1955 Tapio Wirkkala flatware, for Rosenthal, came his way about a year ago, for example. While he was researching the history, he and Pat used it. "It is fabulous," he says. "Every tool is just right for its job. We'll be keeping it."

Ronn didn't grow up surrounded by midcentury modern furniture. "I came at design through a love of cars while I was still an adolescent," he says. He read about the men who designed the cars

Opposite and right: In a bedroom, autographed photos given by Cab Calloway to Ronn's father join family photos on the dresser/desk, designed by Norman Bel Geddes in 1936. The dresser and the chest are souvenirs from 20 years of Ronn's collecting in his American Machine Age/Art Deco period. A quarter-oval mirror on the wall repeats the sweeping curves of the furniture and anchors the display of photos and art. Beside the chest of drawers stands a 1920s "skyscraper" shelf unit inspired by Art Deco architecture.

and learned that Raymond Loewy, for example, was the genius behind the 1963 Studebaker Avanti, as well as the designer of adding machines, refrigerators, the Coca-Cola bottle, the Greyhound bus, and John F. Kennedy's *Air Force One*. The more Ronn learned, the more he wanted to learn, and his study took him, he says, "into more and more objects, then into broader history, more subjects, deeper into the dynamics of cultural symbolism, advertising theory, form versus function, and so on." The passion for design, combined with an insatiable appetite for knowledge, produced the collector and later, the dealer.

Investment**Value**

Mass production—and the U.S. courts' refusal to grant patents for furniture designs—made it easy to copy and then manufacture furnishings at a lower price than the designer-label goods. The result is a market full of imitations, which creates a challenge for collectors. How do you know whether the Eames chair you're contemplating is vintage 1950s or a later version? And does it matter?

To collectors like Ronn, it matters a lot, because one will increase in value and the other won't.

"Vintage pieces that are signed will appreciate much faster than unsigned versions," says Ronn, "unless you are lucky enough to acquire a prototype. The older the piece (closer to original starting production), the better. Good condition is crucial, of course. Most designers insisted that their names be found somewhere on their designs. With Russel Wright, for example, nothing left the manufacturers without his name on it." Ronn adds that some designers, including Charles and Ray Eames and T. H. Robsjohn-Gibbings, weren't as insistent. "Look at the base of a lamp or on the bottom of a chair to find the signature." If there's no signature or label, Ronn launches an enjoyable search through catalogs and books, which leads to conversations with curators and collectors around the world.

The beauty of good 20th-century design is the commitment to suitability for the intended function, says Ronn. "Everything in our home is chosen for its usefulness, beauty, and value over time. We

Repeating shapes

Tight curves on the Modern Age table speed up the sense of movement, while more relaxed curves like those of the sofa slow the pace. Even the glass bowls repeat the curves so that the sense of movement plays out in the details as well as in the overall shapes. With curved shapes dominant in a room, it's important to include some hard vertical edges and rectangular shapes for contrast and balance.

Organic curves

Japanese-American sculptor and architect Isamu Noguchi designed this coffee table for Herman Miller in 1948. Considered an icon of modernism, its biomorphic shape reflects the artist's concern with nature and the distillation of form to its essentials. The wooden legs recall ships' rudders, while the glass top recalls an amoeba.

Slice of life

Officially known as Model No. 437, the "Slice" chairs designed by Pierre Paulin in 1959 have chromed steel legs and molded plywood inner forms that are covered with latex foam and fabric. The French designer studied stone carving and clay modeling in Paris before designing furniture for Thonet and Artifort. His sculptural approach is evident in the ergonomic curves of these chairs. In the 1960s, his work took on the joyous and irreverent look of Pop art.

Right: A blue-green vase by Per Lutken forms part of a still life that celebrates color and sensuous form. The matte finish on the red and gold bottles contrasts with the shiny surface of the green vase, adding another dimension of visual interest.

relax on the Oscar de la Renta sofa, put our food on Russel Wright 'Queen Anne's Lace' dishware, and have meals at the Eames dining set. We hide our television and stereo equipment in a Paul McCobb cabinet and read by Gerald Thurston lamps every day. Only our computers go down in value."

Harmony of form is the key to mixing classic 20th-century modern furniture and accessories with pieces of other periods and styles; it's also key to creating comfort in interiors that are more thoroughly modernist, like Ronn's and Pat's. On another level, how-ever, both comfort and harmony are personal issues that go beyond the visual elements of color, shape, line, and texture. "Harmony is about personal history, personal comforts that have nothing to do with the outside world," Ronn says. Family heirlooms, oddball collections that give you pleasure, certain colors that you love or hate can't be ignored if you hope to find harmony in the home, he says. "Home is, I hope, the one place you can go and probably find some peace. Those homes do not happen by accident. They are created."

"I intentionally juxtapose deep cool colors with the complementary colors of the wooden floors, the wooden furniture, and some of the art and glass. **I want a restful feeling, but not sleepy.**"

Charles and Ray Eames experimented with molded and bent plywood forms to create leg splints for military hospitals to use during World War II. The technology made possible the bent plywood furniture that was designed and produced after the war. Collectors of midcentury modern artifacts usually display the leg splints as wall art; Ronn hung his over a wall-mounted light.

Opposite: A handblown Italian art glass bowl combines satisfyingly hefty mass with an elegantly simple shape. Much of the appeal of glass lies in its transparency, depth, and complexity of colors. Italian glass tends to be created in a more "expressionist" manner, allowing the process to show in the final product.

creating

comfort

comfort is **easy on the body** and the eye, cushioned seats and backs, not too soft, not too firm, just-right ergonomics, livable, convenient, promoting contentment and well-being, **colors** that cheer the spirit, **touchable textures.**

Beth and Robert Sachse,
Tulsa, Oklahoma

"The blend of old and new is important to me. Modern cleans up the traditional look, and the traditional pieces warm up the modern."

mixing classics

"Most modern furniture is shown in a stark setting, and people can't relate to it," says interior decorator Beth Sachse. "They don't think they can have it without getting rid of all their family pieces." Not true, she adds. The home she shares with her husband, Robert, in Tulsa, Oklahoma, is proof. In their 1949 ranch house, modern icons such as the Grand Confort chair and Le Corbusier chaise longue partner with classic rolled-arm sofas, Queen Anne tables, and French antiques. One secret to a successful mix lies in letting one style dominate and using the others as accents. Color also contributes to the harmonious blend.

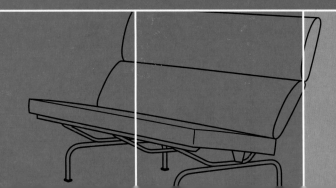

Above: In the family room, Beth stashes the electronic equipment in a French pine armoire. The leather-and-chrome chaise longue (designed in 1928 by Charlotte Perriand, Pierre Jeanneret, and Le Corbusier) offers a relaxing angle for watching the flat-screen television over the fireplace. An antique French mantel frames the firebox.

Left: The black leather-and-chrome chair, designed by Le Corbusier in the 1930s, was revolutionary because it turned chair construction inside out: The steel framework encloses the upholstered cushions. The chair and the Oriental rug are classics that won't go out of style.

Below: An acid-washed and scored concrete walkway spreads like a carpet before the front door of Beth and Robert's 1949 ranch house. Bright green moneywort fills the insets and softens the edges.

Left: Instead of using the fireplace as the focus of the main conversational grouping, Beth chose to make it the centerpiece of a secondary, more intimate seating group. The symmetry of the architecture and the style of the molding on the fireplace surround give this end of the room a decidedly traditional look; the boxy armchairs nudge the attitude toward a more modern, cleaner style. The color of the upholstery echoes the color in a landscape by William Hook. The needlepoint top of the antique bench rounds up the main colors in the room.

Opposite: Every area needs a focal point, says Beth, and here it's clearly the painting by Jason Wheatley. Beth says it's a metaphor for the game of life, with birds stacking precarious piles of rocks. The artist's use of a 19th-century trompe l'oeil style to express a contemporary perspective captures an aspect of Beth's modern-traditional mix. Global influences are evident in the African stools, which serve as side tables to the custom-designed club chairs, and in the Chinese motifs on the cotton Scalamandré sofa fabric. All the woods are dark, which unifies the room; the repeating red elements also help tie the space together.

Beth and her sister, Sallie Hughes, own S. R. Hughes Interior Design. Their decorating business was originally rooted in country antiques, but over the years, they've shifted toward English, then French antiques. Now they include modern classics and contemporary Italian design in their shop. The English-French foundation is still dominant in Beth's home, but it's leavened with modernist influences and freshened with globe-trotting accents.

The living-dining area presents a look of traditional formality that's nevertheless inviting and comfortable. The sofa combines pleasingly plump down-filled cushions and a padded back with shapely rolled arms; the shape echoes the curving knees of the Queen Anne-style side table and the chinoiserie-inspired coffee table. The club chairs facing the sofa have similarly rolled arms and plump cushion backs. All those curves communicate traditional comfortable style.

Across the room, the accent is on contemporary style, with Italian chairs drawn up to a wood dining table, also Italian. On the wall, a large abstract painting makes a stunning focal point. It's paired with a Grand Confort chair, whose scale suits the spot, says Beth. The simple lines of the chair also complement the painting. Into

> *We see these pieces as art. They're not going to go out of style.*

this company she introduced her mother's antique English chinoiserie clock, which dates from about 1820. The pairing reveals an unexpected kinship between the aged patina of the clock and the scarred, layered surface of the painting. In addition, the clock and the table are made of woods that are similar in color. *"Having the clock there is fun,"* says Beth, *"because it loosens the tight feeling. I don't like things to look too modern."* Still, she acknowledges, the clean geometry of modern elements keeps rooms from being too busy. Also, she and Robert have invested in the architect-designed icons that reflect modernist theory. *"We see these pieces as art,"* she says. *"They're not going to go out of style."*

Having plenty of conversation areas is key to the couple's notion of a casual, livable home. *"I like to have furniture arrangements that invite conversation,"* says Beth. *"Every area needs someplace people can perch."* She believes that each area of a room needs a focal point, something to draw your eye and engage you. In the living and dining areas, art is the focal point on three walls.

Above: The moldings and shape of this clock's cabinetry are in the European tradition. The decoration, called chinoiserie for "in the Chinese style," was popular from the early 17th century into the 19th century for everything from furniture to porcelain, wallpapers, fabrics, and garden architecture.

Opposite: To give the dining room a strong focus, Beth framed the Marcia Myers landscape with an antique English chinoiserie clock and a Philippe Starck lamp called "Rosy Angelis." The Grand Confort chair anchors the grouping with a solid block of color, yet doesn't interfere with the painting.

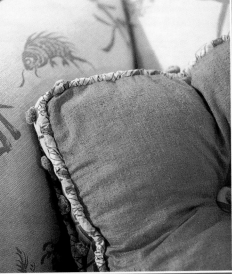

Opposite: In the dining area, Italian chairs covered in leather draw up to a contemporary table. On the other side of the room, traditional-style furnishings dominate. Unity is important in a ranch house, Beth notes, because "you can see from one end to the other. It's important not to have a lot of different things going on." That's why she opted for a minimal palette that's basically monochromatic, with doses of red for warmth. "Red seems to infuse a room with energy," she adds. "Then you throw in the positive tension between fine antiques and modern classics, and you have an exciting space."

Unify with color

"The overriding element that holds everything together is color," says Beth. Red inspired by her Imari collection appears throughout the house. Sensuous red leather chair covers edged with black reveal Italian craftsmanship and quality. Silk pillow fabric repeats the fresco-red pattern on the sofa. Beth doesn't limit herself to a single red; flowers illustrate the range of shades possible, from the peachy pink centers of 'Exotica' roses to the intense, saturated red of gerbera daisies and the magenta of gloriosa lilies. Touches of bright green intensify the red and bring out colors in nearby artwork.

Beth and Robert travel frequently, and their trips have brought global influences to bear on her decorating. African stools made in the 20th century serve as side tables in the living room. "They have a simplicity that works well with modern," says Beth. African objects inspired early modernist painters, such as Picasso and Braque, so there is a historical connection between the two styles, she adds. Asian influences enter by way of wall hangings, furniture design, and a collection of Imari porcelain, much of which Beth inherited from her mother. Touches of Imari red appear in nearly every room in the house, ensuring continuity throughout the home. Carefully weaving together pleasing color, touchable texture, and open space creates an environment of casual ease for the Sachses. You might think achieving such an effect would require careful calculation, but Beth says otherwise. "Like life, I let rooms 'just happen,' rather than planning them formally," she asserts. "We love things that have a sense of humor, that remind us of happy times, or that we have inherited and are sentimental about. When you mix all that up, it's bound to work."

Jerry and
Rebecca Sundt,
Tucson, Arizona

"

romantic modern

To me,
comfort is
style. An old
leather
couch may
feel great,
but if it
doesn't look
good,
it's not
comfortable.

"

Fresh out of college neither Jerry Sundt nor his bride-to-be, Rebecca, was particularly concerned with acquiring furniture and accessories. Rebecca lived with roommates, and Jerry's apartment was furnished with a hodge-podge of hand-me-downs, much as any college bachelor pad would be.

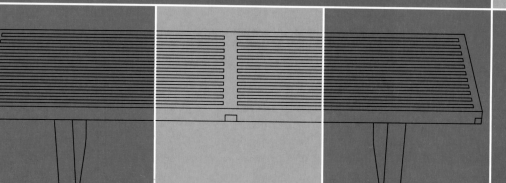

Above and left: Good to look at and great to sit on—that's how Jerry and Rebecca describe their furniture. Los Angeles interior designer Alex Miranda encouraged the couple to invest in pieces with classic or transitional lines so they'd have the flexibility to update by merely changing the upholstery. Contemporary tables combine the brown finish of traditional furniture with a spindle or spool shape that recalls the spiral of an auger seashell. Repeating the medium-dark wood finish on chair legs, tables, and case pieces like the armoire (see page 64) unifies furnishings of different periods and styles.

Below: The couple's pink stucco townhouse, built in the 1980s, reminds Rebecca of Southern California-style architecture.

new**classic**style **63**

When Jerry bought his first home, a 1980s townhouse, things began to change. "We have a friend who is really into modern," says Rebecca, "and he took Jerry shopping in Los Angeles. That's when he found Dialogica." The showroom features the lush new designs of Monique and Sergio Savarese. Elegantly crafted sofas, chairs, tables, and lamps combine global influences with the best of 19th- and 20th-century furniture shapes and lines, freely reinterpreted from a late-20th-century point of view. "They have by far the most accessible modern furniture," says Jerry. "It's good to sit on and it's good to look at. It's contemporary but not cold and stark." One chair caught his eye: a curvaceous piece with lines that recall an Empire sofa, upholstered in golden velvet. It came home with him shortly before he and Rebecca married, and the piece launched the couple on their decorating adventure.

"That chair was his favorite thing in the whole place," Rebecca says. "That was our challenge. We had to find other things to go with it." As they acquired furnishings, one piece at a time, Jerry made most of the design decisions at first. "I think he had more of an idea of the type of furniture and styles he likes. He was set on this look," says Rebecca. She was more inclined to traditional and classic looks. "I like a lot of different things," she says. Growing up in Hiawatha, Kansas, she lived in a house furnished with antiques

Right: A traditional armoire anchors the room with a rustic look that suits the Southwestern spirit of the plaster walls, the kiva-style corner fireplace, and wooden beams (see page 66). Brown wood tables with spindle legs have a transitional look that mediates between the extremes of modernism and tradition. The upholstered chairs play with traditional shapes but exaggerate and streamline them to create contemporary style.

Left: The traditional-looking rolled-arm sofa with arched back captures Rebecca's notion of comfort. To play down its bulky proportions and blend it into the room, the couple covered it in gold fabric. Pillows bring in accent colors of red and blue, which repeat on the bulkhead in the dining area and in the kitchen above the cupboards, drawing the eye from room to room.

Right: A painting by San Francisco artist Eric Zenor was the couple's first joint purchase. The colors anticipated the palette they would settle on for the house, and the style recalls the work of Italian Futurists. The lines in the painting find an echo in the swooping curves of the shelving supports and chairs. The chairs and credenza come from Dialogica. "We're starting to look like a showroom," jokes Rebecca, "but it's hard to get Jerry out of there." The chairs evoke the sleek, organic lines and beautiful finishes of classic midcentury modern work by Danish architect Finn Juhl or British designer T. H. Robsjohn-Gibbings.

Sensuous shapes
Graceful, curvaceous bottles capture in miniature the sweeping lines of chairs, sofas, and shelving supports. These accessories underscore the romantic modern look the couple wants to create.

Anchored in history
Many icons of modernism are still in production or have been reintroduced in the last few years. Mid-20th-century pieces continue to inspire furniture designers. New work that evokes or builds on the past without copying it offers an alternative to vintage modern—and perhaps a chance to invest in new classics.

that her parents bought at auctions and restored. She jokes about being brainwashed into liking contemporary furniture, but Jerry maintains that their decisions were a joint venture. "Once Rebecca got involved, she really got involved," he says.

Starting with the yellow-gold of the chair and the red in an Oriental rug inherited from Jerry's grandmother, the couple settled on a primary color scheme of yellow, red, and blue. They chose a beautiful blue velvet slipcover for the sofa; but, Rebecca says,

"once it was on the couch, it was too much—it was a blue monster." That's when they realized they needed some help. They asked a clerk at Dialogica for a recommendation and were directed to Los Angeles designer Alex Miranda of AM Interior Designs.

"He came to Tucson and looked at what we had," says Rebecca. "We spent a whole day measuring," adds Jerry, "and he took pictures." Working long distance proved not to be a barrier to a successful partnership. The designer sent packets of fabrics and ideas for three different color schemes, with notes identifying where each fabric would look best—on a chair, on the sofa, or at the windows. "It worked really well," says Jerry, "because we could sit down with a glass of wine and think about it. There wasn't that pressure you feel when you're standing in a store trying to decide."

ColorPower

Miranda suggested creating ambience by painting the living room walls a warm, earthy yellow, accented by spicy red on the

Opposite left: With clean lines and an airy design, a brushed-steel table and chairs reduce visual clutter in the modest kitchen. Although the furniture is contemporary, it sits comfortably in the Southwestern-style setting, thanks to compatible textures (frosted steel and glazed tile) and colors (cool gray metal and cool green walls).

Opposite right: Jerry wanted to paint the kitchen walls eggplant, but Rebecca longed for cobalt blue. Practicing the fine art of compromise, they asked the decorative painters for unbiased advice, which they wisely followed: soft green for the walls, cobalt for the soffit, and gold trim between the cabinets. Eggplant went in a small bathroom.

Below right: For furnishing the patio, there's no debate: Contemporary iron chairs and table and a generous umbrella invite outdoor living except in the hottest weather.

bulkhead between the dining area and the kitchen. To open up the windows and soften the architecture, he urged the couple to replace the shutters with draperies. Replacing the blue velvet on the sofa with yellow-gold fabric helped blend the chunky seating piece with Jerry's favorite chair, creating a more harmonious effect. "He also brought in sisal rugs so the room would have a neutral base," recalls Jerry. The Oriental rug moved into the bedroom.

"The challenge is how to make things tie together," says Jerry. "Alex showed us how to do that, and without tremendous amounts of money. He did little things—the color palette, the draperies, some lamps with red shades, and all of a sudden, wow, it works!"

Although most of their major furnishings have a modern or post-modern look, the armoire in the living room (pages 64–65) introduces a complementary traditional note with its crown molding, round pulls, and medium brown stain. The diamond pattern on the front suggests a Southwestern influence that harmonizes with the adobe-style kiva corner fireplace; the color of the wood blends with the wood of the contemporary coffee table. Allowing one style to dominate and introducing a contrasting element as an accent

gives rooms a clearly defined personality—in this case, a style the Sundts call "romantic modern."

The shapes and proportions of the upholstered pieces communicate a come-hither comfort. The gold chair "*is very snug,*" says Rebecca. "*You sit in it and feel safe because of the way it curves in on you.*" For Jerry, comfort has to do with the visual impact, as well as the physical appeal of the furniture. A slouchy leather couch may feel great, but if the proportions and lines are sloppy, it's jarring to look at and uncomfortable to live with. Rebecca has a different perspective. "*I like a lot of pillows that you can float into. I love couches like that.*" Jerry's response: "*I personally don't think that's the most comfortable. Pillows can say comfort, but it depends on the style.*"

Despite their distinctly different notions about comfort, they agree that they have become more closely aligned in their decorating tastes. "*I have come around,*" says Rebecca. "*And I have softened up a lot,*" adds Jerry. "*I've moved away from hard-and-fast modern. We both respect each other's opinions so much that we really enjoy doing this together.*"

modern country

Richard Martino
Sagaponack, New York

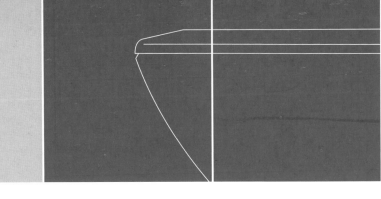

" I don't think about mixing things in terms of styles or periods. If I see a piece and I like it, I buy it. "

Once upon a time, country and modern were style labels
found at opposite ends of the spectrum. Country was dark paneling, Early American-style furniture, rustic finishes, and muted colors. Modern was chrome and steel, blond wood, streamlined shapes, and bright, garish hues. Who would have thought they could find common ground? Richard Martino, for one, although reconciling stylistic opposites wasn't really his goal.

Above and below: The chimney rises from the original part of the saltbox cottage. In summer, a swag of pink roses frames the new entrance, added in 1994.

Left: A new cantilevered staircase leads to the loft and bedrooms. The bent-steel Bertoia chair, with its geometric shape and clean lines, is one of several vintage modern pieces that caught Richard Martino's eye. Behind the sofa, the golden wood of a Heywood-Wakefield chest draws the floor color up into the room, softening the contrast between white walls and black pottery.

Above: In summer, the living room becomes a breezy enclosed porch when screened windows and doors are opened. A pale, neutral color scheme expands the already ample sense of light and space. Generously sized chairs by early 20th-century Parisian designer Jean Michel Frank draw up companionably around an original Heywood-Wakefield coffee table. The weathered texture of a primitive American child's chair (holding a pot of pansies) contrasts with the sleek finish of the coffee table and metal side tables, grounding the room with a touch of antiquity. The simple shape of the antique echoes the straightforward lines of the modern furnishings.

Above: Exposed beams, paneled walls, pine floors, and multipaned French doors and windows create a clean country backdrop for midcentury modern and contemporary furnishings. Painting walls and ceilings the same semigloss linen white emphasizes light and space.

"I don't think about mixing things in terms of styles or periods," says the freelance art director. "If I see a piece and I like it, I buy it. Since it's all coming from me, there's going to be something that makes the different pieces like each other." That something is probably defined by shape and color. Everything that comes home with Richard tends to be streamlined and neutral or light in hue, creating an uncluttered but comfortable look.

White&Light

The reconciling of opposites begins with the house itself. Richard bought the gray, cedar-shingled saltbox in 1982 as a weekend retreat. Located on Long Island, it's surrounded by potato fields and sits close enough to the ocean that Richard can smell the salty air. The interiors were neither streamlined nor light "The first thing I did was tear down the fake beams, sand the floors, and get out my paintbrush," Richard says. He applied linen white paint to the ceilings and walls and left the pine floors their natural honey color, protected by polyurethane. "Maybe it's the art director in me," says Richard, "but I love white. I like the cleanness of it, the way light reacts to it in a room."

The natural light in the house enchants Richard. "The way the light goes through the house has always been the thing I love about it," he says. With the help of architect William A. Schulz, over the last 20 years Richard has added a new master bedroom and dining room, enlarged the kitchen, doubled the size of the living room, and built a garage. Whenever he could, Richard replaced walls with glass, using French doors and 5½-foot-tall casement windows with mullions. The multiple panes are more work to clean, but they're appropriate to the architecture and preserve the country character of the house. Upstairs, in the master bedroom (pages 82–83), he installed glass dormers instead of using solid walls, giving himself unobstructed views.

Opposite: The garden room gathers light from the north and west. The blue-black color of the bluestone floor anchors this cozy space, where upholstered chairs and an armchair from Herman Miller gather around the Danish RAIS stove, designed by architect Bent Falk in 1970.

Right: Originally a tiny galley kitchen, the area now opens onto the dining room. Sandblasted glass doors on the cabinets hide everyday dishes but bring a more open feeling to the room than would a bank of solid doors. The backsplash is glass tiles that have been sprayed white on the back and then mounted on the wall. The glass is easy to clean, and the treatment has the opaque look of milk glass.

"Sometimes I feel like I'm living inside a sundial," says Richard. "I tend to follow the light as it moves through the house during the day: morning coffee in the living room, cocktails in the garden room, wherever the sun is shining." He continues to look for ways to bring more light into the house. "I'm thinking of adding more skylights," he says. "I don't think in terms of overall architecture," he admits. "I want it to serve my purpose, and I figure it will probably look good too."

Pale**Palette**

All the remodeling has created an open, spacious interior that feels as light and airy as an urban loft. But it retains the warmth and friendliness of a country cottage, thanks to beamed ceilings, pine floors, and painted pine walls. To furnish the house, Richard assembled a mix of midcentury modern pieces, generous upholstered chairs, contemporary tables, antique pine cupboards, and antique chairs. He doesn't set out to collect period pieces or vintage furnishings, he says, and midcentury modern isn't a passion. However, he admits that when he was growing up, he was always jealous of

Right: An outdoor deck was enclosed to create the dining room and the garden room beyond it. Richard began collecting Heywood-Wakefield pieces like this dining room set because he liked the streamlined style. The chair seats are covered in a vintage 1920s fabric. The company produced chairs of this design from 1950 to 1955, then introduced a similar but shorter model from 1956 to 1966.

Above: A rustic pine table and contemporary horn chair carve out a work space in the area created by a dormer window.

Opposite: In the guest room, an antique pine table and 18th-century English cupboard provide handy storage. Warm wood, clean lines, and usefulness of these pieces appealed to Richard.

friends who had Saarinen tables. "I thought those kids were totally cool." The Heywood-Wakefield dresser, dining table, and chairs, along with seating by Jacobsen, Eames, and Bertoia, are "just pieces that I buy and then I put them somewhere and move them around. I take each piece on its own merits, in terms of finish, shape, and color," explains Richard.

There is one proviso: "I do take the palette into consideration. If I see something I like but the color is wrong, I won't buy it." Adhering to a consistent scheme of pale wood, shiny chrome,

Basic black
Handmade objects warm up a room, and anything in basic black adds depth and richness. Turned ebony vessels from Africa have basic shapes that suit the monochromatic, minimalist look of a classic modern interior, but they also update a country house. Black pottery from Mexico or the American Southwest can achieve a similar effect.

Industrial accents
Chrome, aluminum, and steel are hallmarks of classic modern design. Using the new materials of industry is part of what motivated modern architects and industrial designers. The Diamond chair, crafted of chrome-plated stainless-steel wire, was designed by Harry Bertoia for Knoll International in 1952. Like certain other icons of modernism, it evoked mass production but actually had to be made by hand.

white paint and fabrics, and neutral sisal throughout the house amplifies the light-filled quality that Richard prizes. It also enlarges and unifies spaces. Black accents—in lampshades, rug borders, pottery, and occasional tables—anchor the light finishes and give the rooms punch. With little or no pattern, rooms feel clean, serene, and uncluttered. Combining clutter-free, light-filled spaces with furnishings that promise casual ease creates comfort that's visual as well as physical. "Broad, open spaces are very comforting," Richard says. "The living room is used mostly for large gatherings,

BRUCE WEBER

but I like to walk through that *space*—it's *tension-releasing* to look at the light."

Richard's goal isn't minimalism but an unfussy simplicity. When you consider that both country style and modernism share an appreciation for simple shapes, a lack of unnecessary ornament, and suitability of purpose, it's not so difficult to see that the two can be compatible after all.

Opposite: In the master bedroom, windows replace walls to maximize light and views. Metal elements—garden tables flanking the bed, a Mexican wrought-iron mirror, even the armillary sphere at bedside—have a clean, linear quality that feels both modern and country.

Above: The antique pine blanket chest doubles as a coffee table in front of a black leather love seat in the bedroom.

" With all of our collections, you'd think the house would be a hodgepodge, but it's not, because of how we display things. It's all about not overloading your senses. "

Becky and Ken Phillips
Dallas, Texas

collector's choice

Don't tell Ken Phillips there are no more vintage Eames pieces waiting to be snapped up at reasonable prices. "We're flea-market-crazy people," he says, "and we've found good prices on things we're willing to dig for. The sofas were used, and we had them re-covered. The rockers on the two rocking chairs had been replaced, and that brought down the price." Another Eames chair they picked up for $30 at a bankruptcy sale at a local bank. Ken's dream, he says, is to have one example of everything

Above: The house, built in 1948, shows the influence of Spanish Colonial architecture, with the sloped edge, arched window, limestone facing, and rough-beam porch supports.

Below: When Ken and Becky found this oak chest about 15 years ago, it was stained "an awful brown," says Becky. They stripped it and pickled it to give it a cleaner look. Tin candlesticks from Mexico and a temple-form antique clock partner with a colorful painting from Mexico for the kind of eclectic (but orderly) mix that Ken and Becky enjoy.

designed by Charles and Ray Eames; the inventive couple's furniture, produced by manufacturer Herman Miller, helped define the look of American modernism after World War II. "*Something special happened when those two people got together,*" he says. "*They were such pioneers and so prolific.*" Along with pursuing Eames artifacts, Becky and Ken also collect Depression-era prints and paintings from New Mexico, Navajo rugs, Native American pottery, and devotional art from northern New Mexico. (They're both from the state, so that inspires the collecting theme.) "*With all of our collections, you'd think the house would be a hodgepodge,*" says

Becky, "*but it's not, because of how we display things. It's all about not overloading your senses.*"

DesigningEye

Ken and Becky are graphic designers, and they approach decorating their home as they would designing a printed page. "*You don't want all pictures or all text,*" says Ken. "*You need design elements and white space. Less is more.*" With this in mind, the couple edits furnishings and accessories in each room to create focal points (the equivalent of pictures on a page), empty areas (white

Opposite: A pair of Eames sofas float in front of the fireplace in the living room, where Ken and Becky listen to music. A concrete-slab mantel rests on rough wood supports, creating a clean-lined focal point. An antique typecase and a Spanish Colonial altar table topped by a folk art weather vane introduce the contrasting textures of worn and weathered wood, a warming counterpoint to the chrome and plastic. The architecture provides warmth as well, with traditional multipaned double-hung windows, shaped molding, deep baseboards, and rough wood beams.

Above left: A WPA mural study by Depression-era artist Peter Hurd stands on the floor, visually balancing the antique windmill tail that hangs on the wall. Additional pieces from the couple's collection of 1930s and 1940s prints rest atop the custom-built bookcase. The Eames rocker is vintage, but the rockers have been replaced; that brought down the price but doesn't diminish the couple's enjoyment of the piece. "People always ask if it's okay to sit on them," says Becky.

space), and transitional areas that connect the two (text). The wood floors are left uncovered, primarily for easier maintenance—the couple has a dog, and rugs tend to accumulate dust and dog hair, both of which exacerbate Ken's asthma. The practical choice also has an aesthetic effect, because bare wood floors unify spaces and reinforce the clean, open feeling created by the furniture placement.

Contrasting**Textures**

In the dining room, metal Emeco chairs (designed for the United States Navy in the 1940s) draw up to a Mennonite table from

Mexico. An oak cupboard stores colorful Navajo rugs and pottery, and on the opposite wall, a contemporary metal buffet holds dinnerware and table linens. A rusted metal weather vane from a Pontiac dealership stands in the corner as sculpture. Ken found it at a swap meet for car parts.

The mixture is eclectic, Becky says, but "if we like a piece, we feel that it will work with everything else we have. I like to mix textures—smooth against rough, cold metal against something warm. We like weathered wood and weathered metal, things that look like they've been knocked around a little." They like to combine these with slick, sleek metals. "It's more interesting than doing all old or all new," she says.

The mix of contrasting textures and of modern and antique pieces works, says Becky, because all the furniture has simple lines. Clean rectilinear shapes and minimal ornamentation have a calming effect, so the furniture doesn't compete with the artwork or accessories. "You don't want the eye to be bombarded," Becky says. Color comes into play as accents: "I like strong color, but not a lot of it. It's there to complement."

Except for the Navajo rugs and pottery, Becky and Ken use very little pattern, which cuts down on visual clutter too. Where they've

Opposite: Lithographs, etchings, engravings, and aquatints depicting New Mexican scenes hang in an irregular grid over a brushed-metal buffet. Ken and Becky chose one example from each artist whose works they own and then arranged the prints according to size, taking care to balance darker images with lighter ones.

Left: A weather vane from a Pontiac dealership stands in the dining room as sculpture. Ken says weather vanes like this were painted bright red and stood on car lots in the open air. The oak cupboard displays a collection of Pueblo pottery and Navajo rugs.

Opposite: Hardwood floors, high ceilings, and an open floor plan give the house a sense of spaciousness far greater than one would expect in a modest 1940s suburban home. The rough timbers that appear in the living room as ceiling beams and mantel supports reappear in the kitchen as brackets under the concrete countertop.

Right: The kitchen was remodeled by the previous owner, a contractor specializing in renovations that update older structures while preserving (or enhancing) the vintage architectural character. Blond cabinetry combines with stainless-steel appliances for a look that's contemporary yet warm.

Weathered wood

A weathered box recalls New Mexican antiques but is a reproduction. Becky likes the crackled paint as a foil for a collection of miniature modern icons. Created for the Vitra Design Museum, the chairs replicate three Eames designs. The white chaise longue, designed in 1948, existed only as a prototype until recently.

Contrasting textures

Brushed aluminum and old wood form an unexpected partnership. The wood's finish is worn smooth from use; the chair is burnished to a satin finish rather than a high gloss. So although the materials—natural versus industrial—contrast, the finishes harmonize. Both the chairs and the table have clean lines with no distracting ornamentation, which further cements the pairing.

created pattern—with collages of prints on the wall—the effect is almost monochromatic: The prints are a variety of sizes and range in tone from sepia to charcoal and black. White mats unify them; silver, black, and gold-tone frames add variety. The prints, which depict scenes of New Mexico, were made in the 1930s and 1940s, many by artists working under the Federal Art Project of the Works Progress Administration.

"I like being surrounded by the things we love and collect," says Ken. "It has taken us a long time to gather these things. I know people say you shouldn't define yourself by what you have, but we don't see it like that. We've surrounded ourselves with furniture and art we love, the scenes of New Mexico, where we're from." The environment they've created produces a level of comfort that makes home their favorite place to be.

A collage of prints hangs in the family room above a table bought at auction from the Santa Fe estate of department store magnate Stanley Marcus. The clean shape and light finish of a new Eames chair complement the table's straightforward lines. On the stair wall, an over-painted print by contemporary Texas artist David Bates introduces a note of ocher into the black and white art collection.

The downstairs family room and a master bedroom above it were added to the house in an extensive renovation that took the interior of the house back to the studs. The builder combined vintage architectural details with a modern open floor plan to create the perfect hybrid: a house rich with historical character but light, open, and suited to modern living. In the family room, a pair of new Eames lounge chairs and a red leather sofa from Roche Bobois form an inviting seating group around the Noguchi coffee table. Ken and Becky's interest in early modernist and regionalist printmakers has led them to begin searching for paintings of the same era, as well as for work by contemporary New Mexican artists, such as the Alyce Frank landscape above the sofa.

> "In my house, the furniture is antique, and the accessories are modern. They contrast, and one grounds the other."

Olivia Cabot
Portland, Maine

color & pattern

Can a 19th-century Victorian townhouse filled with antiques find happiness with draperies and rugs inspired by midcentury modern design? It's an unexpected marriage: Lofty rooms with deep cornices and ornate plaster ceiling medallions seem an unlikely setting for textiles in playful geometric designs. Yet opposites do attract, and this house in Portland, Maine, proves they can make a happy pair.

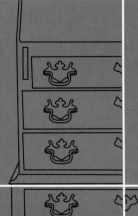

Above and below: Built in 1864, Olivia Cabot's brick townhouse stands on a shady street in Portland's West End. Rope-carved columns, brackets, and scrolling-vine fretwork framing the porch and bay window reflect the influence of the Italianate style, which reached its peak of popularity in the 1860s.

Left: The previous owner installed glass block in the entry to provide privacy while admitting light. Although this material usually is associated with modern architecture, it isn't entirely incongruous in this entry, thanks to the Pop-art wave pattern Olivia had applied to the walls.

The house and its furnishings belong to Olivia Cabot. The textiles are by Angela Adams, widely acclaimed for her rugs, pillows, and fabrics, which evoke the 1950s but don't imitate specific vintage patterns. The two met about 10 years ago during one of Olivia's annual summer visits to North Haven Island, where Angela grew up. "I love her designs," says Olivia. "I had a lot of antiques passed down to me from my grandparents and great-grandparents, and I wanted to incorporate them with her designs." So she asked Angela to help her decorate the townhouse.

DesignExperiment

The collaboration presented them with an opportunity to experiment, and the results greet visitors as soon as they enter the stair hall. From the chair rail to the ceiling, the walls vibrate with a scalloped pattern rendered in shades of blue, brown, and cream. "I wanted to do a mural down the whole hallway," says Olivia. "Angela came up with the design, and I chose the colors. I like the blue and brown. It seems very Art Deco to me." In fact, brown appears throughout the house as a recurring theme in Olivia's decorating and in her own painting. Combining brown with blue represents earth and sky, she says, and she appreciates the way those colors make a room feel grounded.

Above right and opposite: Angela Adams painted the entrance hall for Olivia in a wave pattern. The lively shape is an exaggerated version of the scallops on the antique mirror frame.

Right: A glass-panel door connects the first-floor parlor to the hall, enhancing the sense of openness. A Danish light fixture sculpted from plastic illuminates the hall.

Right: A pencil drawing of Olivia Ames, Olivia's grandmother, drawn by Albert Sterner in 1914, provides a focal point above the Italian marble mantel. Pyramids of Italian ceramic flowers establish dainty symmetrical balance on the mantel shelf. On the wall above, Olivia hung a trio of puzzles that she found at a local shop. The tile-like patterns reflect her interest in tiles and mosaics as inspiration for her own art.

Above: A color scheme of yellow, brown, and white ties together antique and transitional furnishings and the architecture. The love seat, one of a pair that suits either modern or traditional settings, wears chocolate-color linen piped in "Freda" fabric from Angela Adams (the same design that's on the pillows). Solid upholstery gives the eye a place to rest; contrasting piping calls attention to the shape of the furniture and helps reinforce the color scheme.

Above right: The Angela Adams rug brings the color scheme into focus and draws the eye to the iron-and-glass coffee table, a contemporary handmade piece. The sides are figures with arms raised to hold the glass top, and art glass fills the body of each figure.

Right: A silk floral in chocolate and white softens the windows with an airy pattern that enhances the feeling of uncluttered openness in the room. The chocolate theme continues in the leopard print that covers the antique English chair, one of a pair that Olivia inherited. The chair's graceful but clean lines—and the straightforward lines of the side table—allow these pieces to fit comfortably in either a modern or a traditional setting.

> **The antiques are brown, so you have the color of the wood against the textiles. Then the furniture is so weighty and serious, and you have the flamboyancy of color against it.**

Opposite: Beautifully proportioned woodwork painted crisp white sharpens the impact of golden-yellow walls in the parlor and living room. Ornate plaster ceiling medallions and chandeliers crown the stately character of the spaces. To the left of the living room doorway hangs artwork by Olivia, wooden shapes mounted on painted aluminum.

The colors may be calm, but the effect of the pattern in the hallway is lively. By happy chance, the pattern echoes the scalloped frame of an antique mirror hanging at the end of the hall. To contrast with the architecture and accent the wall pattern, Olivia installed a contemporary Danish ceiling fixture. "When it's lit, it's like a floating orb," she says.

Style**Counterpoint**

On the first floor, the living room and parlor form one large, sunny area divided by pocket doors. Angela persuaded Olivia to paint the walls a warm golden yellow. "It casts a great light and it works so well with other colors," she says. "With the beautiful trim in Olivia's house, I thought it would look like lemon meringue—and I think it does." At the same time, they planned for coordinating rugs, pillows, and draperies from Angela's first collection, which she named State of Mind. These designs, introduced in 1998, were immediately dubbed retro modern. "Initially that frustrated me," admits Angela, "because I wasn't sure we were retro-looking. But in essence that collection was inspired by the simple life of the island I grew up on, where things don't change with the trends." Kitchens like her grandmother's are still full of linoleum, Heywood-Wakefield furniture, and dinette sets, she says. Those interiors feed her eye and inform her designs. Collectors of midcentury modern furniture and accessories recognize the affinity between her work and their furnishings. The spunky retro quality and bold colors provide a refreshing counterpoint to the architecture and antiques in Olivia's home.

The living room, which is relatively casual, overlooks the street through the bay window. The adjoining parlor is more formal, with a pair of love seats framing the Italian marble fireplace. Olivia's favorite chocolate brown covers the love seats, and another of Angela's rugs defines the seating group. The love seats anchor the room and provide a solid-color bridge that links textiles of different styles—the modern rug, the stylized-floral draperies, and a formal fabric that combines a leopard print with chinoiserie images. Above the mantel, three small puzzles call attention to Olivia's interest in mosaics, tile patterns, and puzzles, which serve as inspiration for her artwork. Along with silk-screening on fabric, she paints watercolor landscapes and makes tile puzzles.

Opposite: Angela Adams and Olivia Cabot developed the color scheme and fabric palette for the living room and the adjacent parlor at the same time. In the living room, the gentle geometry of the rug and the drapery fabric resonates with the shapes outlined by moldings and floor inlay. At the windows, fabric hangs in simple panels from plain rods; this understated window treatment preserves the room's simplicity and modern feeling. The bay window showcases a table and porcelain jar, Cabot family heirlooms. On the wall to the right are watercolors by Eric Hopkins, a New England artist whose graphic, almost primitive style mirrors the geometrics of the textiles. The table, named Mod Pod by Sherwood Hamill from Angela Adams' company, is new but recalls midcentury modern design.

Right: A chocolate and lemon pillow provides a spot of dark color to anchor the sunny palette in the living room. It also links the room to the adjacent parlor, where chocolate fabric plays a starring role. An antique lamp with a French-glass base injects a complementary accent.

Below right: Inherited antiques mix casually with Olivia's own acquisitions, producing an authentically evolved look. Above the antique English bombé desk hangs a painting by early-20th century painter Marion P. Sloane. Fine art never needs to match the furniture, but the fuchsia silk lampshade accents the red barn in the painting, drawing the eye more persuasively toward the art.

Courageous**Color**

In the dining room (see pages 104–105), Olivia and Angela applied bold tangerine to the walls, then crosshatched it with lavender for a loose trellislike effect. Another of Angela's rugs lays a pattern of magenta and dark gray-purple under the legs of an antique table and chairs. "I like the solidity of the antiques against the textiles," says Olivia. "The antiques are brown, so you have the color of the wood against the textiles. Then the furniture is so weighty and serious, and you have this flamboyancy of color against it." The contrast between the two enhances them both.

At the same time, color knits the room together: A traditional woven fabric on the dining chair seats pulls the wall color into the room; the magenta of the rug reappears as a surprise backdrop for porcelain in the corner cabinet. Using such strong color successfully calls for courage, but choosing hues that draw out the wood

Olivia's fearless juxtaposition of brilliant color and 18th-century antiques defies conventional notions about decorating with traditional furnishings. Pastel portraits of her great-uncle Richard Ames and her grandmother, Olivia Ames, hang above a Federal sideboard. The interior color of the corner cupboard influenced Olivia's choice for the rug. Angela Adams suggested the tangerine for the walls with magenta lines applied freehand for texture and depth.

tones also ensures a satisfying scheme. Undertones of red and yellow in the sideboard and dining table pick up the warm coral on the walls.

Happy**Pattern**

On the second floor, color comes only from the textiles and art, and furnishings are more streamlined and contemporary. In the "blue room," Olivia practices yoga. An abstract painting on the mantel anchors the room with a concentrated dose of color that's echoed by the custom-designed flower-shape velour chairs. The draperies and shag rug (both Angela Adams textiles) bring the blue-and-brown theme of the entry hall upstairs; their patterns infuse the room with a rhythmic sense of movement. Because the walls, mantel, and moldings are painted the same light-reflecting white, the stately architectural details assume a sculptural quality, and the clean backdrop creates an appropriately calm atmosphere for practicing yoga.

Color can play up the architecture or play it down, but pattern is the element that breathes fresh life into each of these elegant rooms. Almost any pattern will produce a busier effect than a solid swathe of color, but Olivia likes Angela's textiles for their simplicity. The modernist-inspired designs and novel hues provide an effective foil for Olivia's family antiques, allowing her to honor her family, she says, by showcasing her heirlooms in a beautiful place.

Opposite, above left, and left: Against white walls, an abstract painting supplies a patch of concentrated color that gives the room a focus. Blue velour chairs pick up the color, presenting happy shapes that harmonize with the spirit of Angela Adams textiles at the window and on the floor. Olivia practices yoga in this room, which is why the Pilates ball finds harbor here.

In the media room, white walls and woodwork allow the pattern of the rug to provide the visual interest as on-the-floor artwork. The thread of chocolate color that runs through the house continues here in the upholstery of the contemporary chair and sofa. The mirror over the fireplace dates from 1800; the crystal chandelier is original to the house. The ornate style of these pieces adds a contrasting flourish to punctuate the geometric simplicity of the Angela Adams textiles. On the wall adjacent to the bay window hangs a watercolor, "Pulpit Harbor Passage," by New England artist Eric Hopkins; the flattened shapes of the landscape reiterate the abstract textile designs.

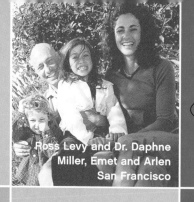

Ross Levy and Dr. Daphne Miller, Emet and Arlen San Francisco

What I like most about our home is the way the house and furnishings speak to the present with a collage of pasts and futures.

comfortable fusion

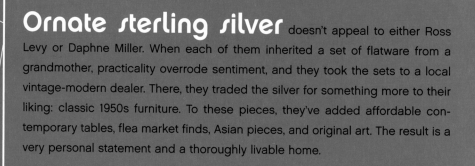

Ornate sterling silver doesn't appeal to either Ross Levy or Daphne Miller. When each of them inherited a set of flatware from a grandmother, practicality overrode sentiment, and they took the sets to a local vintage-modern dealer. There, they traded the silver for something more to their liking: classic 1950s furniture. To these pieces, they've added affordable contemporary tables, flea market finds, Asian pieces, and original art. The result is a very personal statement and a thoroughly livable home.

Above: Influenced by Japanese culture, the family treats the entry area as a point of transition between the house and the world outside. They remove shoes and coats here and stow them on a rack or in the 18th-century tansu chest. Ross Levy designed the wire-mesh balustrade to frame the stairwell that descends to the bedrooms.

Left: Daphne Miller had the glass top of the IKEA coffee table sandblasted to give it a high-end frosted look.

Below: Lime and melon put a festive face on the 1930s house. The colors are historically correct but reversed in their application, with the 1930s trim color as the base and the old base color as trim. Typical of many San Francisco homes, it hugs the sidewalk in front, and the yard drops down below basement level in the back.

VAN BRUGGEN   Frank O. Gehry Guggenheim M

Repurposed lighting

An old operating room light found at a local secondhand shop serves as a sconce in the living room. The fixture, which is glass painted with reflective paint, has an industrial look that adds character to contemporary or vintage-modern settings. Check flea markets and secondhand stores for utilitarian light fixtures. Have them rewired before installing them.

1960s crafts

A type of table lamp popular in the 1960s combined cone-shape fiberglass shades and bendable metal stems that allow light to be directed up for ambience or down for task lighting. Along with the enameled flower arrangement that Ross dropped into the vaselike base, the lamp exemplifies the 1960s marriage of mass production and craft.

Many collectors of midcentury modern flock to online auction houses to pursue the hunt for treasures, but that approach doesn't appeal to Daphne, a physician with her own family practice. *"For me, the thrill is the flea market,"* she says. To those who say no bargains are left out there, she says not so: *"My office is entirely furnished with stuff from flea markets, including the exam table—and I got two bright yellow Herman Miller chairs for $75, desk chairs for $25. You can still find good deals. People either don't know what they have or they don't like it,"* so they're willing to sell at good prices. Daphne also checks thrift shops regularly and finds prizes like the vintage draperies in the dining room.

The mostly modern mix of furnishings reflects the couple's appreciation for the historical significance of midcentury modern style. *"It represents function taken to a higher level,"* says Ross. *"Aesthetics and technique crossed paths at that time."*

Open**Space**

The family's home reflects a creative intersection of old and new. When they bought it, the 1930s bungalow needed major renovation and remodeling; by the time they finished, the boxy, chopped-up spaces had been transformed into an open, airy plan with a spectacular view.

Ross earned his degrees in architecture from the University of California at Berkeley and Harvard University and spent time in Boston doing historical renovation and carpentry, building lofts, and working as a general contractor. That experience shaped his approach to remodeling the house, deciding what to keep of the original structure and what to change. Character-defining elements such as the brick fireplace and coved ceiling with moldings in the dining room stayed; the walls and plaster ceilings in the living room and kitchen were dismantled to open up spaces.

Opposite: A new picture window opens the living room to a spectacular view of San Francisco. Ross and Daphne create comfort by combining vintage Heywood-Wakefield, Eames, and Bertoia chairs with a coffee table from IKEA and a sectional sofa that 4-year-old Emet calls "the art sofa." A painting from the *Self–No Self* series by Korean-American artist Sandra Sunnyo Lee successfully competes with the view to arrest the eye. In rooms with relatively little wall space and high ceilings, art needs to be large and bold to anchor the space and lift the eye upward.

1950s style

The abstract paintings of modern artists such as Pablo Picasso, Joan Miró, and Paul Klee inspired craftspeople working in the 1950s to incorporate abstract or primitive figures into their work. The crafts, in turn, inspired lamp manufacturers, who adapted modernist figure sculptures to mass-produced table lamps like this one.

Intriguing contrasts

Inexpensive copies of Isamu Noguchi's famous light sculptures are limited to simpler forms like the accordion box on tripod legs. The quality of the paper, the shape of the legs, and the complexity and size of the form distinguish genuine Noguchi pieces. If you're not ready to invest but want the effect of soft light and airy shape, imitations offer an affordable option.

Removing the plaster revealed the wood beams and planks that made up both layers of the roof's double-frame construction. Ross added insulation and roofing above the planks and left the old structure exposed in order to gain ceiling height. The effect is rustic yet modern.

The walls, on the other hand, are contemporary in inspiration. Most are Swiss-coffee white, with two important exceptions: "*We use color to signify certain walls,*" says Ross. The center wall is structural, as is typical in San Francisco houses. "*The center wall escorts you down the hall to the living area and the view,*" says Ross, "*so it was important to call attention to it. And I happen to*

The new kitchen opens to the living room and the hall. Ross pierced one wall with a window to create a line of sight to the front door. The stainless-steel table, found at a restaurant supply store, doubles as work space and a breakfast table. The old plaster ceilings in the kitchen and the living room were removed to expose the beams and planks. Now whitewashed, they lay the structure bare—something modernist architects appreciate—yet play on associations with country or rustic architecture.

Above: The family uses the original living room as the dining room. An old pine door, stripped and secured to a sturdy trestle base, serves as the dining table. At each end are signed Thonet chairs found at a flea market. New Italian chairs fill in along the sides, reflecting the continuing influence of midcentury modern on contemporary design. The piece in the corner, an old-fashioned refrigerator, was discovered in a junkyard. Daphne cleaned and painted it to use as a china cabinet and bar.

like lime green. In the bedroom, putting color on the wall instead of using a headboard or canopy creates atmosphere."

The platform bed seems to float in front of the aqua wall, underscoring the serene effect of the color. Renovation uncovered the original Douglas fir floors, which the couple refinished in a warm honey-tone color. A vintage-modern dresser supplies matching warmth, and its straightforward, uncluttered lines echo those of the bed. An area rug introduces lively pattern and color, a jolt of energy in a quiet room.

In the bedroom and throughout the house, strong, boldly scaled, and thought-provoking original art anchors spaces. Ross says they have never set out to acquire art in an intentional way. "In every case, we encountered these pieces somewhat randomly," he explains. "We found them and realized that we needed them—they spoke to us and to our artistic and philosophical sensibilities."

In one way or another, the objects that Daphne and Ross choose for their home have personal meaning. The vintage pieces, says Ross, "refer to a period of time that was hopeful, and they figure into our own personal history, the times we acquired them, the evenings spent with the children, dogs, cats, friends." They aren't static pieces arranged in homage to a period of design history. Emet and Arlen recognize that their house is special too. "They love having a house that is different from most of their friends' houses," says Ross. "They enjoy entertaining company and showing them how we live."

Above: A 1950s dresser from a local vintage-modern shop supplies bedroom storage. The rocking chair belonged to Ross's grandmother. A rough wooden sculpture by Norwegian artist Beatta Rønning Arenson stands sentinel in the corner.

Opposite: The platform bed is from a Canadian manufacturer but has a Japanese simplicity to it that pleases Ross and Daphne. Instead of using a headboard or canopy, they painted the wall a clear aqua; it anchors the room and creates atmosphere. A painting by California artist Amy Donner emphasizes the wall as a focal point.

> "We wanted a home that was very eclectic, but clean and modern in feel. I was particularly interested in combining stylistically contrasting elements.""

a fine balance

Kimberly and Dan Renner
Austin, Texas

Marriage has spurred more than one couple to toss out their hand-me-down furniture and start accumulating new pieces together. For Dan and Kimberly Renner of Austin, Texas, furniture shopping had to be worked in around an even more pressing task: rebuilding a 1917 Arts and Crafts house they'd chosen as their new home. The once-grand residence, located in a downtown neighborhood, had been subdivided into apartments, with a 1950s addition that provided two more units.

Above: In the entrance hall, Kimberly Renner updated an antique chair with a casual tie-on slipcover sewn from white cotton duck. Asian pieces like the bamboo cupboard are style chameleons, blending as easily with traditional furnishings as with modern. To equalize the difference in height between the cupboard and the chair, Kimberly hung an antique painting above the chair.

Below: Artful remodeling turned the 1950s addition into the main entrance and restored the original 1917 structure (at the left) to its Arts and Crafts glory.

Simply functional

Utilitarian objects and industrial materials can serve as a foil for natural materials and decorative shapes. With their simplicity and straightforwardness, items such as these wire baskets stay out of the spotlight and let the eye focus on warm woods and more elaborate furnishings.

Grand gestures

Garage sale finds, the Empire chairs were reupholstered in black leather to match the dark wood finish. The single-color effect emphasizes the chairs' energetic shape and bold scale, which offer a striking counterpoint to the clean-lined stainless-steel tables and office chair. The leopard-print rug repeats the black to anchor the chairs in the room.

Opposite: A stainless-steel restaurant table, found at a salvage yard, serves as the Renners' desk in their home office. The couple likes the juxtaposition of industrial steel and antiques. The no-nonsense verticals and horizontals of the table and rolling medical cart duplicate the vintage-style geometry of the paneling and trim. As a result, the eye goes straight to the curving shapes of the French Art Deco burled-walnut cabinet and Empire armchair, which serve as focal points.

The interiors had been so ravaged by the conversion that the Renners were unable to salvage much beyond some floor boards and bathroom tiles. "We retained the foundation structure, the roof structure, the fireplace, the basement, and the front door," says Dan. "This was not your average renovation; it was a rebuilding."

The project took several years to complete, and during that time, the couple lived in a little garage apartment behind the house. They sold or gave away most of the furniture they'd owned before marrying and began collecting new pieces, storing them until the house was ready.

Inveterate collectors, they regularly shopped garage and estate sales as well as antiques markets. Utilitarian and functional objects, such as industrial or metal pieces from the 1930s, 1940s, and 1950s, caught their eye. A vintage fan, lamp, and office chair were purchased with a home office in mind. Other objects would find new

purpose. "We enjoy finding well-designed objects and adapting them to uses other than what they were intended for," says Dan. Now a wire wastebasket holds architectural plans, metal drawers function as a side table, and old office stools pull up to the kitchen island to serve as barstools. One prized piece is the stainless-steel table that serves as a desk in the home office. "It was salvaged from a used restaurant equipment yard for less than $100," recalls Kimberly. It served as a work table during the rebuilding process, then moved into the office to become a desk. "Talk about bang for your buck!" she says.

Their talent for rummaging has also uncovered the types of treasures that make fellow flea market enthusiasts jealous: Thonet dining chairs, a Florence Knoll love seat and table, a Victorian "energy-gathering device," and assertive Empire chairs were all found at estate sales for very little money. "Both the Thonet chairs

Form and function
Whether 21st-century plastic fans will ever become collectible is open to debate, but appliances from the 1930s and 1940s are collectible precisely because industrial designers attended to form as well as function. This fan, with circles of wire bound by two bands of three wires each, does more than stir air; it looks breezy too.

Intriguing contrasts
The Renners were drawn to this old pine ladder for its construction and patina. The metal wheel under it is a Victorian "energy-gathering device" that they found at an antiques fair. A 20th-century reproduction French armchair proves the enduring appeal of this antique style; cowhide upholstery puts a contemporary spin on the 18th-century shape.

Above: The love seat and coffee table, designed by Florence Knoll, were rummage sale finds, as were the Thonet chairs at the dining table. The rosewood parsons table echoes the brisk, sharp lines of the coffee table. A pastel painting by Will Klem, an Austin artist, adds color between the windows.

and the Florence Knoll love seat were in poor condition when we found them," says Kimberly. The low up-front investment meant they could spring for beautiful upholstery on the love seat and have the chrome finish restored. The savings also allowed them to have the Thonet chairs refinished. These pieces are now some of the couple's favorites.

The modern icons and utilitarian pieces share the guiding design principle of modernism: form follows function. That philosophy, first expressed by late-19th-century Chicago architect Louis Henry Sullivan, ultimately led to glass and brick boxes furnished with chrome, steel, and more glass—buildings and furniture characterized by rigid lines and bare-bones forms. Thus modernism

Above: The Renners mix architectural approaches as well as furniture styles. When they rebuilt the interiors, they created a more open floor plan than would have been typical of the period.

Left: The openness starts in the entry hall, where French doors welcome the backyard inside.

Above and opposite top: "I really wanted to have a generous and functional kitchen and family area," says Dan. The couple centered the island in the room so they can work in the kitchen and still converse with guests in the family room; the high counter blocks views of kitchen clutter. The cabinets were crafted from the same longleaf pine as the floors and capture the style and spirit of vintage Arts and Crafts cabinetry. Paneled wainscoting and beaded-board siding for the island also evoke period style. Modern pendant lamps illuminate the island.

Right: A plate rack, old-fashioned latch-style hardware, and glass doors give kitchen cabinets a vintage look.

Left: Kimberly paired a hefty upholstered chair and an Indonesian teak "lazy chair" in one corner of the family room seating group. Both chairs have high backs, and the front legs thrust forward at the same angle, so they balance each other. To tone down the legginess and mediate between the two shapes, she added a side table configured from metal drawers. The drawers had been attached to the restaurant table that now serves as a desk in the office; the Renners detached them and added a wooden top and metal casters for feet.

Columns mark the transition from the master bedroom to the sitting room, formerly a sleeping porch. Sheer fabric hung from the ceiling turns the bed into a romantic room-within-a-room.

Opposite: The 1950s rattan and teak love seat was an estate sale find. White pillows add comfort and serene color.

The metal chair frame
was a flea market find.
Kimberly intended to
have it covered in
leather, but she liked its
sculptural quality so
much that she decided
to leave it bare.

acquired a reputation for being cold, hard, and uninviting. Now, decades later, the Renners and others are finding that attending to function doesn't have to mean sacrificing comfort and warmth.

Period Style

For the Renners, the architecture of the house helped achieve that feeling of comfort. In rebuilding it, they wanted to capture the spirit of the original 1917 house. Kimberly, formerly the manager of a city recycling program, was committed to using salvaged materials. Although there was little to save from the original structure, she says, "I did not want to put new material into an old house." Dan was less enthusiastic at first. "I didn't want to salvage," he confesses. "Now I am as zealous about it as she is." The original pine floorboards downstairs were too badly damaged to leave in place, but the Renners found a company that salvages beams from demolished industrial buildings and milled them into 2¼-inch-wide longleaf pine boards. The couple installed the boards throughout the first floor. "Their subtle waxed shine reflects light beautifully, and their warm color always makes the house seem sun-filled," says Kimberly. In the new, open floor plan, the floors provide the primary unifying element tying spaces together. New kitchen cabinets were also crafted from the same longleaf pine; the couple couldn't find salvaged hardware, so they chose hand-made oil-rubbed bronze latches and hardware that looked old to maintain a period feel.

"Stripping and refinishing the interior paneled doors was a huge pain," says Dan, "but it was worth it." Reusing the old crystal doorknobs saved money and preserved some of the character of the house too. Kimberly sorted through the original downstairs floorboards from the dining room and set aside the ones that were

Left: The Renners added built-in drawers, cupboards, and shelves behind the bed. The beaded-board paneling and vintage-look hardware create period style.

Opposite: In an area formerly occupied by three small apartments, the Renners built a large closet and dressing area and a master bath, connected by a mirrored hall.

worth keeping. These were bleached and used upstairs in the master bedroom and bath. The master bath turned out to be Kimberly's favorite room in the house. Because they were gutting and rebuilding, they could customize the floor plan to meet their needs, she says. So three small apartments upstairs became a luxurious master bedroom suite, with a large closet, dressing area, and master bath. "My husband and I don't need to get ready for work at the same time," says Kimberly, "so while he gets dressed in the morning, I visit with him in the bathroom. I designed the room to accommodate a comfortable chair and a table for my coffee cup." They also installed two sinks and included a cast-iron footed tub and a separate shower.

Throughout the house, new architectural details designed by the Renners faithfully evoke the style of original Arts and Crafts interiors: In the hallway and living room, flat molding divides walls into a grid that resembles paneling. In the office, kitchen, and family room, high paneled wainscoting gives dimension to the walls. Beaded-board paneling wraps the sides and back of the kitchen island in keeping with the vintage-style cabinets. In the early 20th

> "This house has just the right mix of contemporary with antique. **It's an inviting home. People seem to want to be here.**"

Opposite: Floorboards were salvaged from the dining room and bleached, then installed in the new master bath. The couple included two sinks, a cast-iron clawfoot tub, and a separate shower. The tub came from a camp where Dan was a counselor in the 1970s. To let in as much light as possible, they left the windows uncovered and had the glass sandblasted to admit light while providing privacy.

century, however, woodwork would have been stained, and the walls would have been painted in deep earth tones. The walls and woodwork in the Renner home reflect a contemporary preference for light-reflecting off-white that leans toward beige, with trim a shade lighter. Windows are bare or minimally treated to take advantage of garden views. As a result, the interiors feel anchored in history but lighter and brighter in keeping with modern tastes.

"Most people think this is still an old house," says Kimberly. Dan agrees that the salvaged materials and the couple's attention to detail help the house feel its proper age. The eclectic mix of furnishings adds another layer of richness, with textures and time periods combining in a visually exciting balance. Antiques resonate with the period architecture; mid-20th-century industrial and commercial pieces introduce an element of surprise. "This house has just the right mix of contemporary with antique," says Kimberly. "It's an inviting home. People seem to want to be here."

creating

serenity

serenity permeates **balanced, centered, elegant spaces** blessed with quiet neutrals, uncluttered openness, infinite vistas, **room to breathe; serenity is** peace, tranquility, stillness, freedom from agitation, bliss, a sense of refuge.

Boyce Moffitt and
Lee Pomerance
Chicago

" I think you can have more fun with a mix. Strictly modern or strictly Victorian seems flat to me. "

future classics

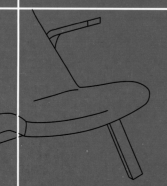

Lee Pomerance grew up surrounded by midcentury modern furniture. "My parents were into the newest looks, but they wouldn't buy anything unless they really liked it," he recalls. "So as a result, our house was almost empty for many years!" Eventually, his grandmother moved in, bringing her fine (but ornate) antiques, which filled out the living room. Being exposed to both traditional and trendsetting design on a daily basis gave Lee an appreciation for each. That early influence is still apparent in his current home, a loft he shares with Boyce Moffitt.

Above: Eames chairs were the natural choice for the dining table Lee Pomerance designed; it combines a base from IKEA and a glass top. The bowed shapes of the table's legs and top support repeat the shape of the chair legs. Introduced in 1945, these chairs were a radical departure from traditional construction because the back support is separate from the back legs.

Below: The Handlesman Lofts occupy the old Handlesman piano factory and store in Chicago's River West neighborhood. Clad in terra-cotta tiles, the building's exterior features neo-Gothic decoration, one of several revival styles that were popular for commercial buildings in the late 19th and early 20th centuries.

Hardwood stairs lead to the den, which doubles as an office and guest room. A natural-pine armoire that would say "country style" in another setting offers clean lines and warm golden color to this contemporary space. The Cube chair and Tube floor lamp behind it are contemporary pieces with midcentury modern roots. The acrylic table, designed by architect Robert Kirkbride, can also serve as a seat.

Occupying most of the top floor of an old piano factory in Chicago's River West neighborhood, the loft boasts 10 windows that are 10 feet tall and extend across the width of the building. Ceilings soar to 14 feet, and ceilings and walls are white—not off-white or cream, but pure white. "In my last place, every wall was painted and finished, and it was darker," says Lee. "I wanted this place to be white and let the color come from the art. It's a big change, but one I like a lot."

In spite of the expansive space, "you don't feel lost in it," says Lee. "The height of the space makes it feel open, but the colors and materials are warm, so I find it very soothing and relaxing. When we entertain, people feel at home and comfortable here." The warm neutral palette starts at floor level, with golden hardwood floors. The wood furniture ranges in tone from honey to blond; sofas, chairs, and the Chinese rug stay within a narrow range of neutral tones as well. The lack of contrast creates a calm,

Opposite: Loft living makes entertaining easy, says Lee, because the kitchen is always accessible. They can serve a few people at the dining table or a crowd seated around the room. White kitchen cabinets tie seamlessly into the white walls of the living area and of the guest room above. The backsplash is tiled in a mixture of grays, greens, and rose, pulling accent colors from the living room into the kitchen. Above the cabinets, white platters and crocks and clear glass vessels create a serene, pattern-free display that relies on shape and texture for interest.

Right: This table, designed by In House and dubbed Circle 3, is crafted of maple plywood. "I just fell in love with it," says Lee. "It looks as though it was designed in the mid-20th century. It is incredibly functional and also looks like a piece of sculpture, different from every angle." He sees it as versatile too, fitting into a traditional setting as well as a modern one. The print on the club chair also evokes midcentury modern design.

quiet mood. Horizontal lines—in the sofas, the buffet, and the block-printed silk piece above it—lower the focus to human scale, so you don't feel overwhelmed by the space.

Lee collects antique Steuben glass, which he displays on glass shelves. The American-made, handblown lead-crystal vases, bowls, and goblets are pale or clear, enhancing the light-filled quality of the room. "This glass is by Frederick Carder, the founder of Steuben Glass Works," says Lee. "I started collecting this back in the late 1980s. I love the variety of colors, shapes, textures, and techniques, all created by the same artist."

The glass collection supports the quiet palette; other art brings enough contrast to give the rooms energy and focus. Over the fireplace, a large mixed-media piece by Chicago artist Kermit Berg arrests the eye with bright color and bold scale. Antique tables made of rich, dark woods flank the fireplace and accent the light woods. On each table, Lee and Boyce mix modern, antique, and Japanese objects. Most of the antiques are family pieces or have personal meaning. "I like the play of the antiques with the modern," says Lee. "But as you can see, none of the pieces that I have are what I would call ornate antiques. They have very simple,

Opposite: A warm neutral palette and an emphasis on horizontal lines induce a serene feeling in this light-filled loft. Blond wooden blinds control the sunlight pouring in through 10-foot-tall windows and tint the space with a golden hue.

Above left: Lee showcases his collection of antique Steuben glass in an Italian cherrywood-and-glass case. The case disappears so that the vases and bowls appear to float. Pieces are arranged so that height and shape vary, leading the eye up and down across each shelf. Color provides visual connections from one shelf to the next. Frederick Carder invented a variety of techniques for creating colored glass; these pieces predate 1920. After the 1930s, the company made only clear glass.

Above right: Club chairs upholstered in neutral linen are comfortable but lightweight and easy to move to the main seating area to accommodate a crowd. Otherwise, the chairs define a cozy conversation nook in the corner.

Opposite: One strong vertical element, a mixed-media piece by Chicago artist Kermit Berg, contrasts with the horizontals to create a dramatic focal point. Framed in industrial steel and incorporating found objects, the piece records a conversation the artist had with his grandmother about loss. Along with antique Steuben glass, Lee collects contemporary pottery. The black vase on the hearth is by Jonathan Adler, whose work has helped define the modern ceramics movement. On the coffee table are two handmade vases by KleinReid, a contemporary ceramics firm.

Below left: An antique cherrywood drop-leaf table fills the niche on one side of the fireplace. The Japanese vase is one of a pair Lee received from his grandmother. Asian pieces mix well with modern, says Lee, and here they underscore the color scheme.

Below: This display juxtaposes old and new design traditions: A contemporary glass vase picks up the color of an antique Japanese plate. The sculptural lampshade, made of white birch veneer, glows with a golden color similar to the antique table's polished finish.

clean lines, and the tables are of good wood." The drop-leaf table is a family piece, and the French demilune table was found at an antiques shop. "They are nice pieces of furniture no matter when they were designed," says Lee. "And that is what I like about them. I think they add a lot of warmth to the room." The antiques bring texture and depth to a setting that is primarily contemporary.

A few of Lee's pieces are midcentury classics—notably, the Eames dining chairs and a Noguchi lamp on a corner table—but most are new designs rooted in mid-20th-century materials and shapes. "I always liked more modern pieces," says Lee. "Midcentury modern pieces were very avant-garde when they were made. I like the idea that pieces being made today are

Harmonies of line

Like the other furnishings and accessories in the loft, the vintage tea service is graceful but restrained in shape, without elaborate surface ornamentation. The Japanese vase offers a similar classic simplicity that works well in either modern or traditional settings. Vases designed by Eva Zeisel for KleinReid (opposite) take such shapes a step further, distilling, squeezing, and re-forming them into playful, organic, sensuous vessels.

Contrasting textures

Vases and other objects created by influential designer Eva Zeisel were intended to delight the eye and please the user with their organic and tactile qualities. Lee displays these on a mosaic table in a sunny corner of the loft. A Noguchi lamp illuminates this intimate spot at night. The lamp's crinkly paper shade provides pleasing textural contrast to the table's glass tiles, the matte-finish vases, and the handblown glass bowl from Copenhagen.

Above: A block-printed natural silk piece by Kermit Berg stretches almost 22 feet along one wall of the loft. The repeating pattern and natural, neutral colors create a soothing effect, and the piece ties this area together. Light-colored wood pieces and linen-covered chairs keep the effect clean but inviting. Lime green and black accents add depth and zest to the pale palette.

extremely modern now and will be classics in the future." The shop he and Boyce own, No Place Like, offers an edgier mix than the furniture in the loft, with more plastics, acrylics, and metals, but they do incorporate examples of each into their home.

In the dining area, for example, a brushed-metal table base from IKEA supports a glass top designed by Lee. He had the edges of the glass sandblasted to enhance the industrial look. He then had to find suitable chairs. "When I started looking for chairs, I kept coming back to the Eames chairs," he says. "They're so comfortable—you can sit in these chairs for hours and you don't feel it. So they were a natural choice, really." Visually, they're the perfect choice, too, blending seamlessly into the setting.

Gleaming hardwood floors create golden warmth from the ground up. The sofa back defines a hall space that leads to the dining table. Above the kitchen cabinets, the ceiling and skylight in the guest room are visible.

Lee had the edge of the glass tabletop sandblasted to suggest industrial influence. The fused-glass piece on the table is by Kathleen Ash, one of Lee and Boyce's favorite artists. "Kathleen doesn't like a flat surface of glass," says Lee. "She doesn't want it to sit; she wants it to rock and have a natural shape."

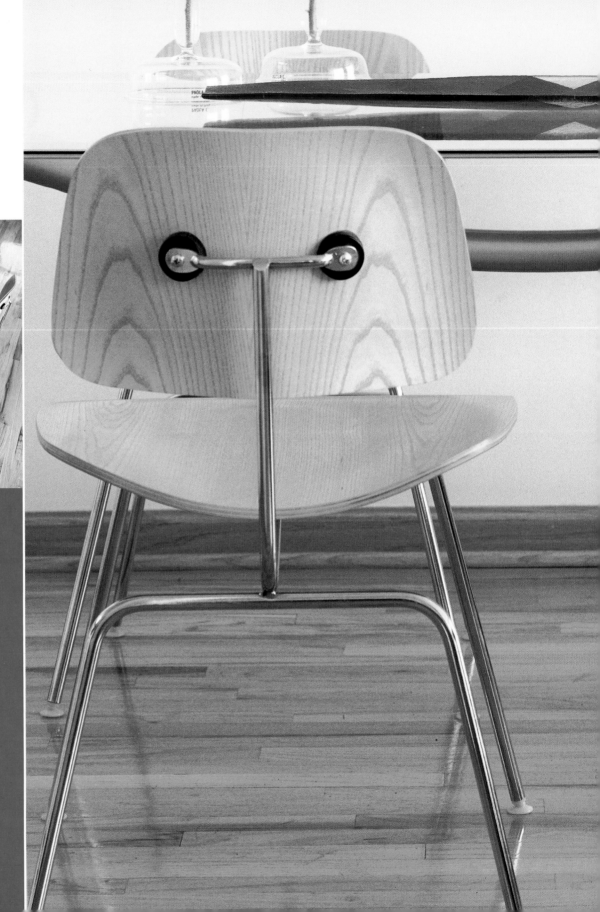

> **"** I like very modern design, **but it's got to be comfortable and inviting. "**

The office/den is behind the kitchen and raised above it on a sort of mezzanine level (see page 137). In it, a pine armoire holds the television and stereo. The pale wood and traditional style of the piece anchor the space and provide a pleasing foil for a new vinyl-upholstered chair and acrylic table. The mix works, notes Lee, because the maple legs on the chair harmonize with the color of the pine; the white vinyl upholstery—a soft, high-quality, low-maintenance material—blends with the white walls.

The acrylic table is a multipurpose piece designed by New York architect Robert Kirkbride. "His whole concept for urban living is to make every piece multifunctional," says Lee. "You can sit on this piece or you can use it as a table, and you can take it apart and put it away if you need to. Most of the pieces we have in our store are like that: clean and simple. We don't have any 'over-the-top' designs. We look for classic modern that makes sense."

In the bedroom, the bed interprets a classic four-poster in steel. Its open design helps keep the room feeling spacious. "And it also shows off the height of the loft," Lee notes, "because you can see that it doesn't go anywhere near the ceiling." A French-style armoire in a rich brown stain anchors the space with the comforting tactile quality of wood.

"I really love a very modern look," says Lee, "but I do like the history of that design and where the look comes from too. So when I find pieces that complement, I like to mix. I think you can have more fun with a mix. Strictly modern or strictly Victorian seems flat to me."

Opposite: "This room was pretty cold before we put in the armoire," says Lee. The dark, rich wood and French-style paneling of the piece balance the lines of the steel bed. On the bedside table, the metal tube is a lamp made from aluminum; it casts ambient light up as well as out through the rings. Beside it is a Jonathan Adler vase, called *Aorta*. Kermit Berg digital photos hang above the bed, perfectly framed by the posts and top rail.

I love modern but I also love the lush, comfortable vintage look. I'm always editing to create a minimal look with antiques, and bringing in modern elements adds excitement.

Liz Zamadics
and
Karl Trollinger
Houston, Texas

becoming modern

"I struggle between the two: the clean simplicity of modern and the coziness of the eclectic or vintage style," admits Liz Zamadics. Her natural inclination toward a clutter-free environment pushes her to pare down possessions and carve out open, minimalist spaces in the 1935 bungalow she shares with husband Karl Trollinger. Her decorating tactics offer textbook lessons on how to nudge traditional interiors toward a more modern—and serene—look. Liz's strategy revolves around incorporating a few carefully chosen accessories and furnishings in each of her rooms.

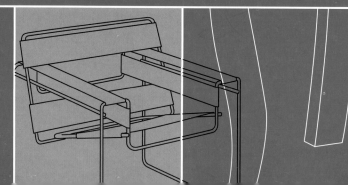

Above: Metal angle-arm table lamps supply modern lines and focused light. Liz Zamadics restricts her wall art to black and white photos taken by her brother. Presented in white mats and plain black frames, they bring a restrained and sophisticated look to the walls. They work well whether Liz decorates in a traditional style or pushes the look to a modern mode.

Left: In addition to editing her accessories carefully, Liz chooses objects that are visually lightweight. Clear glass vases and silver photo frames provide shape and sparkle without crowding surfaces or creating clutter.

Below: Built in 1935, this Houston bungalow combines traditional architecture with an open floor plan.

In the living room, sitting room, and sunroom, cushiony uphol-stered pieces announce put-your-feet-up comfort. Although the shapes are traditional, a dress code of tailored white slipcovers gives them a neutral personality that can be contemporary or tra-ditional, depending on what Liz pairs with them. To keep the white from tiring the eye, she introduces new pillows from time to time. When she wants to push the mood toward modern, she chooses pillows in graphic designs and dark solids.

White slipcovers also simplify and soften the 19th-century French chairs in the living room. Liz likes the chairs for their tall profile and the dramatic contrast between the scrolled arms, legs, and stretchers, and the crisp rectangles of the backs and seats. To bal-ance the height of the chairs, she flanked the sofa with a pair of tall contemporary floor lamps. In the "valley" between the seating pieces, she pushed together two low black corner tables from IKEA to serve as a coffee table. "I liked the simplicity and sharp lines of the tables," she says, "and the black anchors the room."

Liz keeps accessories to a minimum, constantly removing items to see if she can live without them. For artwork on walls and man-tels, she uses only black and white photos by her brother, Stephen. They're matted in white and framed in plain black, to make the most of their clean, graphic quality. Mirrors, clear glass vases, and silver boxes and bowls add sparkle without fussiness or clutter. Liz chose not to dress the windows with fabrics, because the material could make the rooms feel crowded and heavy. Instead, white

Opposite: An uncluttered, graphic approach to decorating creates a modern mood even when some of the style-setting furnishings are antiques. A neutral color scheme and well-edited accessories evoke the serenity Liz craves. She added floor lamps and parsons-style tables to an essentially traditional setting to push the fresh, clean-lined look further.

BEFORE

Left: Liz expressed her traditional side by using an antique drum table as a coffee table, a table lamp with a flared black shade, and neutral pillows. White upholstery updates the French chairs; the outline of brass tacks is a traditional decorative touch.

Above: Pieces with simple lines create a clean look. Silver bowls and boxes have a long history as elements of traditional style, but their sleek shapes blend them into a modern setting. Polished silver and satiny lacquered tables also make harmonious partners; a sculpted and varnished cross adds complementary rustic texture.

Left: In a small room, Liz finds that using a few distinctive, large-scale pieces rather than many small ones creates coziness without crowding. To keep the neutral color scheme interesting, she layers touchable textures, including chenille, velvet, sea grass, silk, and fake fur. The textures of brick, tile, and pottery also contribute to the palette. The slipper chair is a typical choice for Liz: She looks for classic shapes and suitable scale that can work in a variety of rooms. She found this one at a thrift shop for $40. "It was covered in orange velvet," says Liz, "but I saw those curves and thought, what a great chair. The scale is good for my house." The chair has worn three different coverings since she bought it.

Opposite: Silver, glass, chrome, and black accessories invoke the textures of industrial materials, giving the room a modern edge.

Above: A bed of cast-iron lattice under the glass top adds depth and interest to a contemporary dining table. In keeping with the principles of modern design, exposed construction is part of the aesthetics of the piece.

Above: A wooden table with turned legs and carved details gave Liz's dining room a traditional personality, even though slipcovers masked the traditional character of the chairs.

wooden blinds fit inside the window frames, providing privacy and light control while showing off the architecture.

BasicBlack

In the dining room, slipcovered chairs pull up to a contemporary glass-topped table with a cast-iron base. Lamps with black retro-inspired bases, a classic black urn, black chandelier shades, and black decorative closures on the slipcovers supply high-contrast accents that keep the eye dancing around the room and reinforce

Opposite: To give her dining room a more modern look, Liz replaced the wooden table with an iron-and-glass one. She also covered the long server in front of the windows with a tailored, floor-length skirt. The fabric helps eliminate some of the legginess in the room and turns down the traditional emphasis another notch. Liz's mother made slipcovers for the dining chairs to give them a more clean-lined look. The closures are for show; the covers slip on over the backs and seats. The chandelier was a junk store find that Liz dressed up with strings of crystals from a lighting store. A fabric sleeve masks the chain.

the visual link between the dining and living areas. "I just love black and brown" says Liz. "Black has a contemporary feel and makes a room stronger. If you place black sparingly around a room, it grounds it and keeps the eye traveling."

Although it's a small house—only 1,600 square feet—it feels spacious, partly because of the open floor plan (a modern innovation inside a traditional architectural shell) and partly because of Liz's decorating choices. A neutral color scheme for walls, furnishings, and floors creates a feeling of flow throughout the house and enlarges the sense of space. Khaki-colored walls make a warm, quiet background for crisp white woodwork and upholstery. The bedroom has beige walls, but white upholstery, black accents, and sea-grass rugs maintain continuity.

"When you're working with lots of white, everything has a kind of flatness," says Liz. For an antidote, she chooses fabrics with a

Top left: In the sitting room, the black metal table, swing-arm lamp, and stacked photographs offer an edgy clean-lined look that balances the plump, comfy shapes of the chairs and ottoman. Slipcovers outlined with piping and skirted with pleats instead of ruffles look casual but not fussy.

variety of weaves, from cotton duck to damask, adding throw pillows in silk, chintz, and even soft fake fur for more textural contrast. Noting that *"shiny is a texture too,"* Liz chooses high-gloss paint for woodwork, and glass and metals for tables and accessories. These elements catch and reflect light and contrast with the flat-finish walls and nubby sea-grass rugs.

Affordable**Update**

"I love to play with decorating," says Liz. Her full-time job as a personal trainer and owner of an exercise studio, The Train Station, keeps her busy, but she pursues decorating as a hobby and enjoys helping her friends. Karl gives Liz his blessing to do what she likes with the house, but she says that, like her, he appreciates the modernizing touches. *"I have fun changing it out, bringing in things to give it a more modern look. It gets me out of my box,"* she says. The tables, floor lamps, and bedside lamps all came from IKEA. *"It was an inexpensive way to update. I spent maybe $300 to $450, and it gave the house a fresh, sharp look.*

"If it were all one thing, it would be predictable, flat, stuffy," she continues. *"It's more interesting if a midcentury modern piece is next to something from the 18th century. It's about shape and form. Old things can look modern in a spare setting, and when you add modern pieces, it feels congruent."*

Opposite: The low-contrast combination of beige walls and white woodwork wraps the bedroom and sitting room in light. White upholstery and bedding melt into the envelope of space, allowing the notes of black to stand out with graphic clarity. The result feels crisp, uncluttered, and contemporary, even though the architecture and the upholstered pieces are traditional.

Bottom left: Liz uses flowers to breathe life and warmth into every room. "This is my weekly pleasure," she says. "I might not have groceries, but I make sure I have a bouquet of whatever is in season."

<blockquote>
"I really love the mix of old and modern together. I like to use the antiques like pieces of artwork.
</blockquote>

Greg Mewbourne
Birmingham, Alabama

high impact

If you grew up in 1950s suburbia, "elegant" and "ranch style" might not be terms you'd expect to find in the same sentence. Yet elegance is precisely what interior decorator Greg Mewbourne has achieved in his 1953 ranch-style house in Birmingham, Alabama. Using a neutral palette, venerable antiques, and manor-size wall hangings, he has imported an old-world richness to the one-level house. Modern seating and contemporary lamps keep the antique tables, tapestries, and paintings from feeling too heavy, and Greg's exercise of restraint in accessorizing emphasizes his policy of using "less, but better."

Above: Slabs of Indiana limestone frame the fireplace, replacing the original, carved-wood mantel. The clean lines and flat surfaces promote the feeling of uncluttered simplicity that Greg Mewbourne seeks. Against such simplicity, the twist-turned legs and carved frame of the antique needlepoint fire screen stands out as art. Gas balls in the fireplace instead of logs look clean and sculptural.

Left: Deeply carved scrolls accent the straight lines of the antique server. Cut glass sparkles under the lamplight as an antidote to expanses of dark wood.

Below: Long, low lines characterize mid-1950s ranch houses, reflecting their roots in Spanish Colonial and Prairie-style architecture.

Right: Classic modern chairs designed by Ludwig Mies van der Rohe fit easily into a setting dominated by fine antiques. The sweeping arcs of tubular steel offer an invigorating contrast to the straight lines of the antique server. The black leather seats and backs punctuate the brown tones of the server and the tapestry; black accents around the room further ground the neutral scheme and give it satisfying depth.

Opposite: A three-part tapestry covers one wall of the living room, warming the space with old-world personality. It's a fitting backdrop for the antique server, which is unusually tall and has a zinc-lined drawer in the right side. The black metal clock (an old family piece that still keeps good time) pulls the accent thread of black to the end of the room. The table in front of the windows displays Greg's collection of Herend porcelain.

"I like keeping surfaces clean, not too cluttered," he says. "I went through that phase of clutter, with every surface filled, but now I'm enjoying paring down. It lets things speak more loudly and makes things look more important when you have fewer of them. There's less confusion."

In fact, Greg's house illustrates how a few high-impact statement pieces can bring a room into focus, and instead of squeezing the

sense of space, actually make the room feel grander. In the living room, framed English tapestries and a 19th-century server anchor one end of the room. That European character is underscored by a Victorian needlepoint fire screen and an antique table with turned legs and a dark oak finish. To balance these visually weighty items, Greg arranges a minimalist seating group in front of the fireplace. A pair of tubular-steel and leather chairs, designed by

Opposite: To enlarge the sense of space, Greg raised the opening between the living and dining rooms and added a matching one between the dining room and kitchen. Varnished floors that originally had an orange cast were stripped and stained dark brown to contrast with white walls and woodwork. Dark wood furnishings repeat the wood tones for balance. The red finish on the antique grandfather clock brings the color of the dining room draperies into the living room.

Ludwig Mies van der Rohe in 1927, faces a new love seat whose straight lines and transitional style work with either modern or traditional furnishings. A pale sisal rug lightens the dark floors and pulls the room together.

The dining room contains only the essentials—a table and chairs—so even though the table is large enough to comfortably seat eight, the room doesn't feel crowded. One huge antique painting on the wall and the Queen Anne style of the table (which is new but made from salvaged old wood) give the room a definitively traditional character. For a leavening complement, contemporary chairs made of molded polypropylene and steel gather around the table, and a silvery beige sisal rug covers the floor. On each side of the dining room—at the windows and across the wide opening to the kitchen—cotton velvet draperies hang in a fresh-ground cinnamon color. The hue punches up the brown and white scheme, and the soft fabric encloses the room in a toasty cocoon.

In both the living and the dining room, Greg uses wall sconces instead of recessed lights or downlights; the sconces enhance the effect of the chandelier and table lamps. "Wall sconces give a warmer light, like lamplight," he says. "At night, the sconces put out the most interesting glow, and you don't even know why the room feels so good, but it's the way light washes the walls."

The rooms feel airy in spite of the grand focal points because Greg has pared down colors and patterns as well as objects. Except for cinnamon-color draperies in the dining room, the palette is limited to white, black, beige, and dark wood tones that range from brown and red-brown to black. The neutrals relate to one another, creating unity, and the strong light-and-dark contrast keeps them from being bland. Pattern has been banished from upholstery and floor coverings, eliminating a potential source of busyness.

The architecture itself was Greg's ally in creating quietly sophisticated interiors. Ranch houses usually have 8-foot ceilings, simple baseboards, plain woodwork around windows and doors, and no

Opposite: The English table, made in the Queen Anne style from reclaimed old wood, is 7 feet long and 5 feet wide, filling the room but not overwhelming it. Polypropylene stacking chairs originally designed for office use serve as comfortable dining chairs. They're visually lightweight to balance the heaviness of the table and painting. Hand-forged bronze wall sconces wash walls with a gentle glow.

Below: In the kitchen, cork replaced old vinyl flooring, and granite countertops replaced plastic laminate; the cabinets are original, repainted dark gray. Upholstered stools can be pulled up to the worktable for quick meals. The table is English, made of reclaimed wood; the drawers run all the way through so they can be pulled out from either side.

Working with high contrast

Strongly contrasting neutrals such as black and white, or espresso brown and white, are classic combinations that create quiet elegance. Layering contrasting textures—old leather, new vinyl, old tapestry, alabaster, metal—and contrasting shapes—a classical urn, an angular contemporary lamp, an ageless round mirror—enriches the high-contrast color scheme with warmth and variety.

Colors of wood

Dark brown woods against white walls provide a thread of continuity throughout the house. A painting by David Kidd and a few carefully chosen objects pick up the rich red-brown tones of the Chinese altar table; the grouping forms a striking secondary focal point in the bedroom. The lamp, a new piece, tweaks Tiffany style by using real shells instead of stained glass.

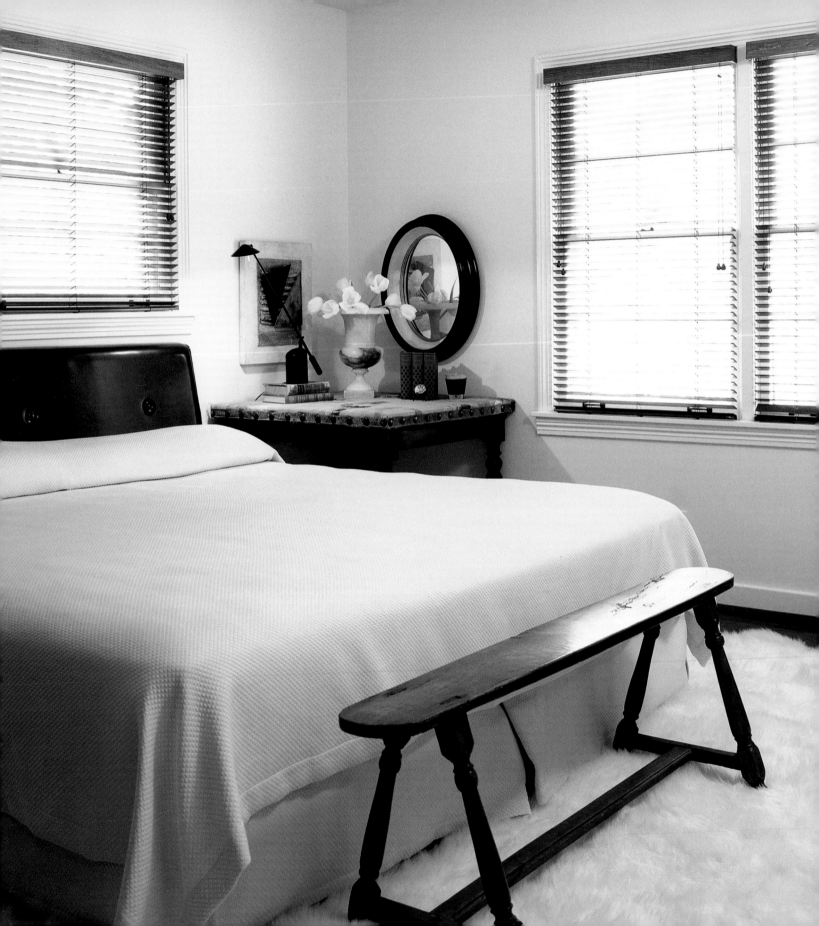

Opposite: A custom-designed headboard is covered in vinyl that has the buttery texture of leather. It tilts at the perfect angle for reading in bed. The wall opposite the bed (not shown) consists of closets and built-in drawers, so storage furniture isn't necessary. The antique bench at the foot of the bed might have been used in a tack room. An ultraluxurious sheepskin rug pampers the toes and enriches the palette of textures in the room.

Right: Greg replaced the original 4-inch-square, two-tone green tiles with 1-inch-square white ones for a stylish vintage feeling.

crown molding. In renovating, Greg says, "I tried not to change the bones of the house. I wanted to keep things true to the spirit of the house and its period." His changes, both structural and cosmetic, amount to a reinterpretation and updating of the mid-1950s look. Varnished floors were stripped and stained dark brown. Interior doors were replaced with ones of the same style but in a darker stain. The woodwork around doors and windows isn't wide but has a traditional profile; baseboards are modest and functional. Instead of emphasizing the woodwork by contrasting it with the walls, Greg bathed walls, woodwork, and ceilings in white.

Greg made the most radical changes in the bathrooms. One featured 4-inch-square ceramic tiles in two shades of green; the other had pink tiles with black trim and inset designs. "I thought about leaving one of them original," he says, "but I just couldn't do it. The

designs were crazy cuts to form zigzags, and in the shower was an explosion of 'starbursts' that was just horrible." In the master bath, he replaced the two-tone green tiles with 1-inch-square white ones on the floors and walls, stopping 10 inches below the ceiling. The new toilet and sink have clean lines and a vaguely European look; the overall effect feels comfortably vintage without evoking a specific decade.

Quality in craftsmanship and materials matters a lot to Greg, and he admits that he's obsessive about details. "I tend to like things a little more finished and stylish," he says. When the details aren't right, he feels uneasy. Happily, this house has met and even exceeded his expectations. From the exterior, with its long, low lines, to the clean, uncluttered interiors, Greg's home radiates a feeling of consistency, and that makes him content.

Cliff, Dylan, and Donna Welch
Dallas, Texas

"

The goal is to look to modernism for inspiration, not imitation.

"

modern gem

It's not surprising that an architect would be drawn to a classic modern house built in 1954. Appreciation for the modernist mandate—simplicity of form and integrity of materials—is built into architectural training. That doesn't mean that Cliff Welch and his wife, Donna, want to live in a cliché. The little gem of a house they discovered needed work, so they restored it—without being slavish. "We wanted to preserve the design intent but adapt it to fit today's lifestyle," says Cliff. "We also made a conscious effort not to fill it with 1950s furniture."

Above: Red doors contrast with wall colors throughout the house, recalling the color-grid paintings of 20th-century Dutch artist Piet Mondrian. Cliff Welch says, "With a modern house, if everything is fairly crisp, there's maintenance involved to keep it that way. If you have a 3-year-old who has friends come over to play, touch-up painting is a part of life."

Left: Chairs designed by Alvar Aalto in 1938 reflect a Scandinavian tradition: the art of graceful lines combined with the technology of laminating and shaping wood.

Below: Built in 1954, the house is an exercise in modernist geometry. Yellow panels and a tiled platform beckon visitors toward the entry, but the cobalt blue door isn't revealed until you approach it directly.

Although most 20th-century modern furniture shares certain characteristics—such as clean lines, industrial materials, and lack of embellishment—there were several stages of development, beginning in the late 1920s. The earliest pieces exploited tubular steel. Scandinavian architects experimented with bent and molded plywood in the 1930s; and after World War II, American designers investigated everything from stainless steel to plywood to plastic and other synthetic materials.

Instead of adhering to the 1950s style of the house, Cliff says, "We really wanted to go for a more timeless look." To achieve that goal, he and Donna selected icons of early modernism and mixed them with contemporary and handmade pieces. In the living area, a pair of Alvar Aalto armchairs, designed in 1938, face a contemporary Italian sofa across a George Nelson bench, designed in 1947. An Isamu Noguchi lamp stands in the corner as sculpture, and a painting by Cliff makes an eye-catching focal point on the blue

Left: Light enters most rooms in the house from two directions. In the living area, the back wall is entirely glass and opens to the screen porch through a 10-foot-wide sliding glass door. Down the hall, high windows admit light from the courtyard into the bedrooms. The white oak floors had been stained an orange-brown; the Welches had them stripped and sealed, preserving the light-enhancing natural color. A sisal rug that's about the same tone as the floors unifies the spare seating group without calling too much attention to itself.

Opposite: Originally, the living room wall was painted baby blue and the doors to the bedrooms and baths were red, yellow, or black. "We deepened the colors to go with the natural brick," says Cliff. "We always thought that with all the natural materials, this wall needed a little punch to it." They had the original drawings, he says, "but even at that, we were guessing whether the colors were those the architect had chosen or the clients. So we used our own judgment."

Right: The platform bench, designed by George Nelson in 1947, can serve as a coffee table or as extra seating. It was produced by Herman Miller until 1967. As design director of Herman Miller for nearly 20 years, Nelson had a profound impact on the production and dissemination of modernist design for both residential and commercial use.

wall. The furniture appeals to them, says Cliff, because of its straightforward shapes and lines, the honest construction (points of assembly are allowed to show), and the way the form and structure of furnishings developed from architectural principles (such as cantilevered construction) and the demands of mass production.

The bold blue wall in the living room draws visitors from the entry foyer into the main living area. Once there, the feeling of spaciousness expands exponentially, thanks to the open floor plan and a glass wall that overlooks a courtyard, screen porch, and the woods beyond. The 20-foot-long glass wall contains a 10-foot-wide sliding door that opens to the screen porch. Cliff appreciates the careful planning that went into designing the house. "There are so many times, whether in the evenings in summer or a nice day in January, that we can sit out there and enjoy the breeze and the sounds," he says. "When we open the sliding glass door, the whole house becomes a screen porch."

Above: Built-ins were common in 1950s houses. This shelf doubles as buffet and display space in the dining area.

Above right: Natural materials such as brick and walnut give the modern house unexpected warmth, says Cliff.

Opposite: Birch cabinets (barely visible at the left edge of the photo) separate the dining area from the entrance hall, but the dining and living areas form one continuous space. Windows along the front of the house are translucent up to 7 feet, admitting light but providing privacy. The top portion of the windows is clear, offering views of the treetops. Cliff made the dining table, which at 7½ feet provides ample space for gatherings of friends and family. The couple found the Cesca chairs at a garage sale.

The Welches prize that connection to the landscape and the quality of light entering the house. Cliff also enjoys people's reactions to the house, because it's not what they expect of a modernist dwelling. "It's not plastic and laminate or steel and glass, but brick and wood, simple natural materials that give people a feeling of comfort they're not expecting."

To enhance that feeling, Cliff and Donna chose furnishings and floor coverings in natural textures—smooth wood, nubby canvas, coarse sisal, and woven cane. Art and accessories are arranged carefully and sparingly to preserve the feeling of openness. The result is a serene expansiveness. "Sometimes just getting rid of a lot of clutter and doing something simple elevates things," Cliff says. Decluttering comes naturally to him: "Order is inherent in architectural training."

In the dining area a built-in shelf eliminates the need for a buffet. Cliff made the dining table, using a base from an office-furniture store and a slab of clear maple. Classic Cesca chairs (designed by Marcel Breuer in 1928) provide comfortable seating.

Modern**Instincts**

"I grew up in a very traditional country-English-style house full of antiques, with something on every inch of wall space," says Cliff.

Below: "We gave Dylan what we felt was the best room in the house because the windows come all the way down to the ground and the room looks out into the backyard and the bamboo," says Cliff. "He gets up in the morning and raises his own blinds to look for the raccoons and squirrels."

"Our house is as far from that as you can get." Cliff's appreciation for modern architecture developed in college, and it grew while he was working for one of the leading modernist architects in Dallas. He remembers visiting his grandfather's office as a child and recognizing that being in that kind of clean, open, functional space felt good. Although Donna's background doesn't include art or architecture, Cliff says, "We've been married 14 years, so our tastes have grown together, and the house really reflects both of us."

Restoring Style

Working together to renovate and repair the house, the couple made a few changes, such as moving the laundry hookups from the kitchen to a hall closet and replacing the kitchen's white vinyl floor with cork. Most of their efforts went into restoring surfaces to pristine condition. "My wife and I are both particular about things," says Cliff, "so instead of painting over old paint, we took walls back to the original surface." However, they didn't necessarily return walls to the original colors. The exterior panels, for example, turned out to have been daisy yellow and aqua. "Even though those were trendy 1950s colors, we felt the house was more about classic modernism," says Cliff. So they chose richer, earthier versions of yellow, blue, and red to use inside and out.

The Welches bought the house from the daughter of the original owners; so they knew that it had been designed by Dallas architect Glenn Allen Galaway for a structural engineer and his wife, a weaver and silversmith. Cliff and Donna didn't know who Galaway was when they spotted the house, but they knew the building was special as soon as they saw it.

The long, horizontal lines and open interiors have been compared to the early work of Philip Johnson. Gridlike planes of color indoors and out recall paintings by Piet Mondrian, as well as the Eames Case Study House in California. The Welches' renovation and research have introduced Galaway to a wider audience, and in 1999, the house received the Dallas AIA 25-Year Award for "significant and enduring architecture." In 2000, the Welches received the Preservation Dallas Achievement Award. That recognition is a happy bonus; the main reward is the pleasure of living in a place that, as Cliff says, speaks to both the mind and the heart.

Opposite: The screen porch brings the outdoors inside (but not the bugs). Cliff and Donna revel in being able to let breezes and birdsongs flow into the house through the open sliding glass door that separates the porch from the living room. Their enjoyment of this outdoor room has led Cliff to encourage his clients to include such a space in their homes. "You have to change your thinking a little bit," he says. "You may not be out there in August, but you can pretty much be there the rest of the year."

guide to classic shapes

The following illustrations show a few possible combinations of modern and traditional shapes. A visual dictionary follows, identifying some of the basic furniture styles Americans use in their homes. International sources are so rich and varied that this section can't cover all of them, but use this guide as a starting point to help you pinpoint shapes similar to furnishings you already own—or would like to own. Then follow the principles of repetition and variety to create your mix.

Ideas for Mixing and Matching

In addition to partnering congruent shapes (curved with curved, rectilinear with rectilinear), pay attention to visual weight and scale. Choose chairs that appear equally heavy—or equally lightweight—so they will balance each other. Match the heights of chair and sofa backs, too, so they are nearly equal. Include contrasts to keep the room interesting: If most of your furnishings are curvy, bring in an armoire or table with straight lines to anchor the room. If most of the furnishings are geometric, introduce a more organic accent piece to soften the hard lines.

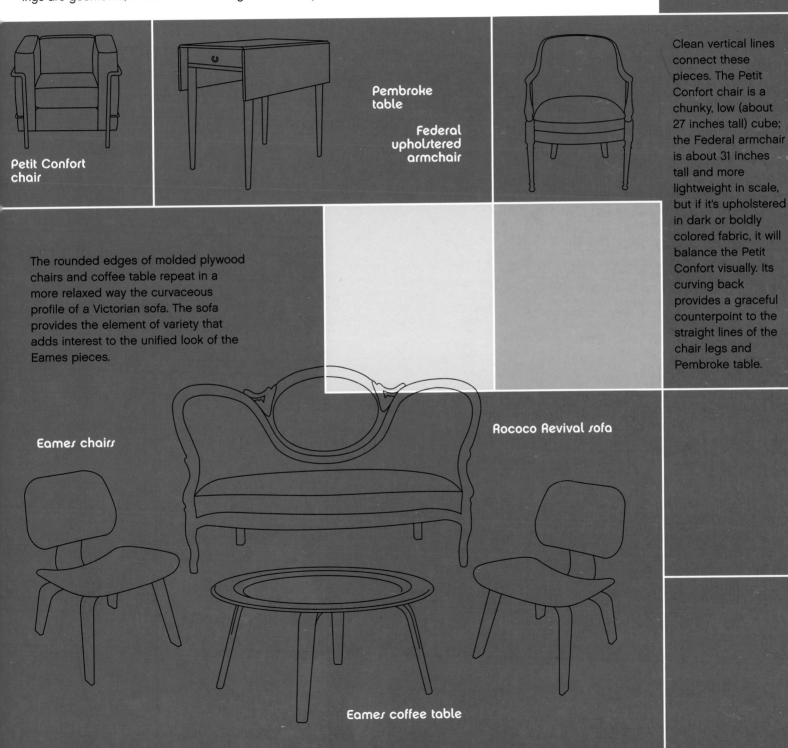

Petit Confort chair

Pembroke table

Federal upholstered armchair

Clean vertical lines connect these pieces. The Petit Confort chair is a chunky, low (about 27 inches tall) cube; the Federal armchair is about 31 inches tall and more lightweight in scale, but if it's upholstered in dark or boldly colored fabric, it will balance the Petit Confort visually. Its curving back provides a graceful counterpoint to the straight lines of the chair legs and Pembroke table.

The rounded edges of molded plywood chairs and coffee table repeat in a more relaxed way the curvaceous profile of a Victorian sofa. The sofa provides the element of variety that adds interest to the unified look of the Eames pieces.

Eames chairs

Rococo Revival sofa

Eames coffee table

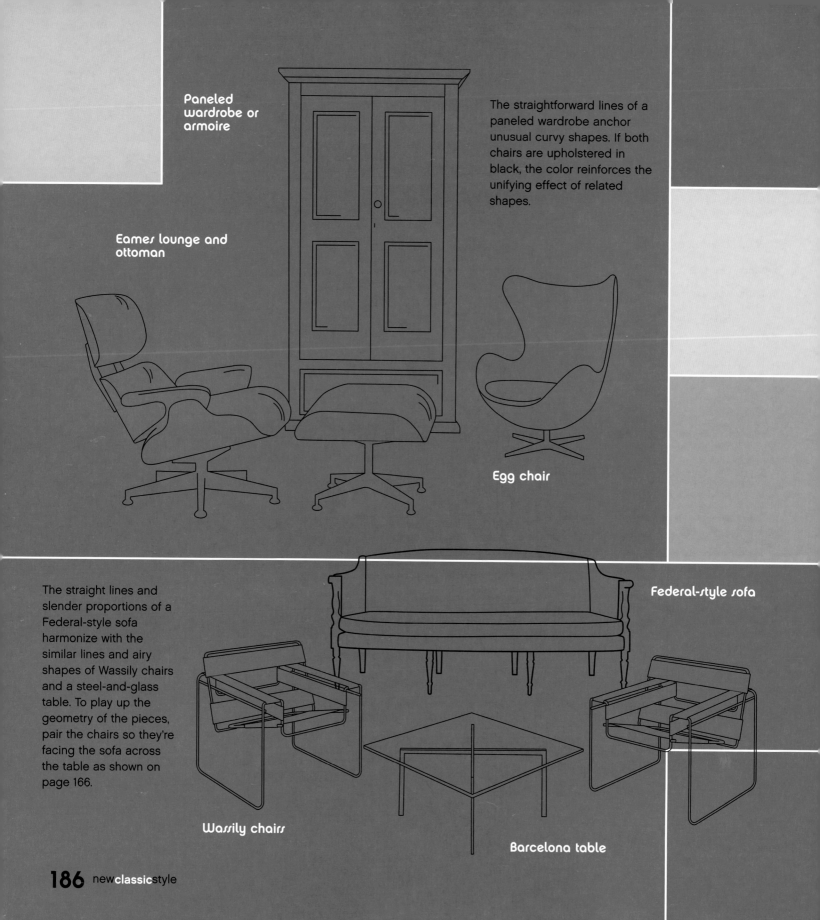

Paneled wardrobe or armoire

The straightforward lines of a paneled wardrobe anchor unusual curvy shapes. If both chairs are upholstered in black, the color reinforces the unifying effect of related shapes.

Eames lounge and ottoman

Egg chair

The straight lines and slender proportions of a Federal-style sofa harmonize with the similar lines and airy shapes of Wassily chairs and a steel-and-glass table. To play up the geometry of the pieces, pair the chairs so they're facing the sofa across the table as shown on page 166.

Federal-style sofa

Wassily chairs

Barcelona table

Chairs

Until the late 1500s, chairs were only for the rich; ordinary folk sat on stools or benches. By the 1700s, almost anyone could afford a chair of some type, and for the wealthy, artisans lavished their skills and creativity on graceful forms with beautiful finishes. In the 20th century, chairs—more than any other furniture type—have inspired architects and industrial designers to experiment with new materials and novel forms and to aim for new heights of artistic expression.

Eames LCW Chair
Designer: Charles and Ray Eames
Date of design: ca. 1945
LCW stands for Lounge Chair Wood; the DCW (Dining Chair Wood) is slightly taller. The birch-faced molded plywood seat and back, mounted on a bent-plywood frame, resulted from the Eameses' wartime research into shaping plywood multidimensionally. Their goal was to create an ergonomically designed chair that would be comfortable without padding or upholstery.

Thonet No. 14 Armchair
Designer: Thonet Brothers
Date of design: 1873–1874

This bentwood armchair was introduced 15 years after the side chair, which was Thonet's best-selling model. Intended for use in cafes and restaurants, it was adopted by early modern architects for residential use; they appreciated the clean lines. Company founder Michael Thonet pioneered mass production of bentwood furniture. After the patent expired in 1869, his designs were widely copied.

Chieftain Chair
Designer: Finn Juhl Date of design: 1949
Modern in conception, with a leather-upholstered seat and back that appear to float above the rosewood frame, the chair was executed by craftsman Niels Vodder in a limited edition of 78. Juhl's early work was for exhibition at the annual Copenhagen Cabinetmakers' Guild shows rather than for commercial production. Most pieces were later reissued for widespread distribution.

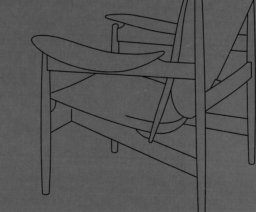

Mission-Style Easy Chair
Designer: Stickley Brothers
Date of design: 1900–1915
This plain, rectilinear oak chair was made by machine but featured exposed tenons and pegs in homage to the principles of handcraftsmanship promoted by the late-19th-century Arts and Crafts movement.

Butterfly Chair
Designer: Jorge Ferrari-Hardoy
Date of design: 1938

Inspired by a 19th-century wooden folding chair, this design—leather seat suspended on a bent-metal frame—has been widely imitated. The official version is manufactured by Knoll.

Wassily Chair
Designer: Marcel Breuer
Date of design: 1925–1928
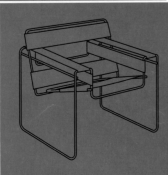
The first chair ever made from bent tubular steel, this classic design reflects the lingering influence of the Dutch De Stijl group on Breuer's early designs. The original 1925 model underwent several changes before Breuer was satisfied with this final version. It was designed for the home of artist Wassily Kandinsky, who taught at the Bauhaus with Breuer. It became known as the Wassily chair in the 1950s.

Panton Chair
Designer: Verner Panton
Date of design: 1959–1960

This stackable chair interpreted in plastic the cantilever principle, which the early modernists had applied to wood and tubular steel. It was the first continuous-form injection-molded chair ever created. The technology to make it didn't come along until 1968. Early models were brightly colored with a high-gloss finish; current models have a satin or matte look.

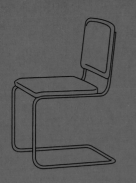

Cesca Chair (Thonet B32)
Designer: Marcel Breuer
Date of design: 1928

Breuer wasn't the first to apply the architectural technique of cantilevered construction to a tubular-steel chair, but his design became the best known and most widely produced. The wood-and-cane seat and back are bolted to the steel frame.

Cherner Chair
Designer: Norman Cherner
Date of design: 1958

A skinny, wasplike waist, sweeping arms, and attenuated legs elevate this chair to the level of art. Designed for Plycraft, the molded laminated wood chair was produced until 1972. Cherner Chair Company has reissued it.

M1554A Side Chair
Designer: Heywood-Wakefield
Date of design/production: 1956–1966

This side chair is one of many variations on the "friendly modern" theme introduced by the consumer-oriented company in the 1950s. Most had light finishes that ranged from wheat to honey.

Eva Chair
Designer: Bruno Mathsson
Date of design: 1934

The bent-plywood legs and arms suggest the energy and grace of a deer; the animal inspiration recalls 18th-century cabriole legs. The solid-wood frame supports a seat of hemp webbing. On a similar model, Mina, the legs and seat frame are continuous.

DAR Chair
Designer: Charles and Ray Eames
Date of design: 1948–1950

One of the goals of consumer-oriented modern designers was to devise chairs with interchangeable parts. This molded fiberglass-reinforced polyester shell could be matched up with a wire "Eiffel Tower" base (shown), a wire-cage base, steel-rod legs, wooden dowels, a cast-aluminum base, or rockers. The shell was designed to be ergonomically comfortable. The six original colors were gray-beige, elephant hide gray, lemon yellow, seafoam green, parchment, and red.

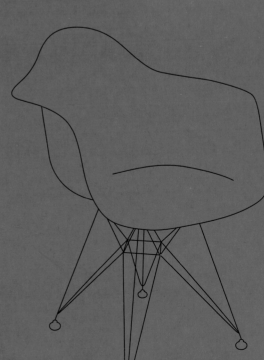

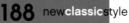

Louis XV Fauteuil
Period: 1723–1774

"Fauteuil" is the French term for a chair with an upholstered seat and back and open arms. Developed from formal state furniture that stood against the wall, the *chaise à la reine* version featured cabriole legs

on hoof feet, arm supports that repeated the curve of the leg, and a square, flat back. The cabriole chair is similar but with a curved back.

Series 7 Chair
Designer: Arne Jacobsen
Date of design: 1955

Originally released as a molded plywood seat on tubular-steel legs, this highly popular chair is available in colorful plastics too.

Swan Chair, Model No. 3320
Designer: Arne Jacobsen
Date of design: 1957–1958

Jacobsen designed the Swan and the Egg chairs for the lobby and reception areas of the Royal SAS Hotel in Copenhagen, Denmark. The molded-foam upholstery shell represented cutting-edge technology.

Womb Chair, Model No. 70
Designer: Eero Saarinen
Date of design: 1947–1948

Designed in response to Florence Knoll's comment that she was "sick of those chairs that hold you in one position," the upholstered, molded fiberglass seat flares to allow for lounging. A Knoll exclusive, it's still in production.

Coconut Chair
Designer: George Nelson
Date of design: 1955

Originally made with a steel shell and fabric-covered foam, the chair was heavier than it looked. Herman Miller has reissued the chair with a lighter-weight molded plastic shell and black leather upholstery.

Grasshopper, Model No. 61
Designer: Eero Saarinen
Date of design: 1946–1947

Saarinen's first chair for manufacturer Knoll apparently didn't sell all that well, but the clean lines have the same energy as Mathsson's Eva chair. Use the wood tone of the arms and legs as a guide to choosing antique partners.

Egg Chair, Model No. 3316
Designer: Arne Jacobsen
Date of design: 1957–1958

Both the Egg and the Swan were created for commercial use, but the sculptural, organic shapes inject a breezy, playful attitude into residential interiors too. A molded fiberglass shell padded with foam and covered with fabric or leather sits on a swiveling aluminum base. The Egg qualifies as a lounge chair—it's tall enough to support the head. Jacobsen also designed an ottoman to accompany the chair.

Barcelona Chair MR 90
Designer: Ludwig Mies van der Rohe
Date of design: 1929

Inspired by an antique source—a Roman magistrate's stool—this chair became an icon of modernism after its debut in the German Pavilion at the 1929 International Exposition in Barcelona.

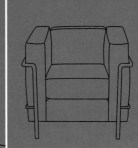

Grand Confort, LC2
Designer: Le Corbusier, P. Jeanneret, and C. Perriand
Date of design: 1928
This design turned the conventional armchair inside out, with the support structure (bent tubular steel) on the outside and the cushions on the inside.

Diamond Chair
Designer: Harry Bertoia
Date of design: 1950–1952
Modern materials—vinyl-coated or chrome-plated steel rods— are bent by hand to make Bertoia's signature-style chair. It's also available upholstered, as well as in a high-backed version called the Bird.

Lounge Chair No. 670 and Ottoman No. 671
Designer: Charles and Ray Eames
Date of design: 1956
One of the most recognizable examples of modern design, this lounge chair and ottoman combine industrial technology with old-fashioned comfort. The prototypes were displayed at the Museum of Modern Art in 1940, and the first chair and ottoman were made for the Eameses' friend Billy Wilder, the Academy Award-winning film director. Original models featured button-tufted black leather cushions on molded plywood shells faced with rosewood veneer. When rosewood became unavailable, manufacturer Herman Miller switched to cherry and walnut veneers.

Rococo Revival Balloon-Back Side Chair
Period: 1840–1870
Based on 18th-century Louis XIV and Louis XV furniture, Rococo Revival dominated mid-19th-century style. Laminated woods—rosewood, mahogany, or walnut—were used to create realistically carved ornament, including flowers, leaves, scrolls, and shells. Most chairs had cabriole legs; the balloon-shape back was popular for side chairs.

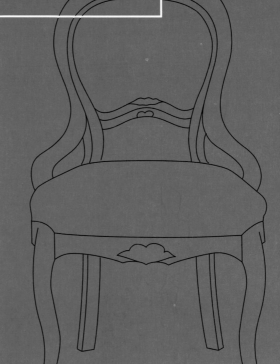

Federal Upholstered Armchair
Period: 1790s
The modified tub or barrel shape of this chair was inspired by Louis XVI bergères; its design descendants can be found in 20th-century pieces by Jacques-Emile Ruhlmann and Philippe Starck. The top rail continues down each side to form the arms, which connect to freestanding, fully turned baluster-shape arm supports. The chair is small (31 inches tall), so pair it with chairs of similar height and delicate scale.

Chippendale Easy Chair
Period: 1730–1765
Based on 17th-century English versions, winged easy chairs were bedroom furniture. The tall back supported the sitter's head; the wings blocked drafts. The Colonial Revival style brought wing chairs into living rooms.

Chippendale Side Chair
Period: 1750–1780

Named for cabinetmaker Thomas Chippendale, this style features cabriole legs, a yoke-shape top rail with "ears," and an intricately carved back splat. Ball-and-claw feet, based on the Chinese symbol of a pearl clutched in a dragon's claw, were popular in America longer than in England.

Empire Side Chair
Period: 1810–1840

Drawing on Greek and Roman forms, the Empire style reflected Napoleon's imperial aspirations. Based on the Greek klismos chair, Empire side chairs feature slender, saber-shape legs without stretchers. The top and middle rails curve to conform to the back and may be carved with classical motifs.

William and Mary Side Chair
Period: 1690–1725

Named for England's reigning monarchs (1689–1694), the style is a late version of European Baroque. A tall vertical profile and blocky turned stiles, legs, and stretchers give the furniture of this period a heavy look compared to the later Queen Anne and Chippendale styles. The cresting rail is elaborately carved; the back is fitted with balusters in the example shown here, but chairs with cane or leather-upholstered backs were also made.

Federal Shield-Back Side Chair
Period: 1800–1820

The shield back, with many variations on the carving of the splat, and the square leg are most often associated with English cabinetmaker George Hepplewhite.

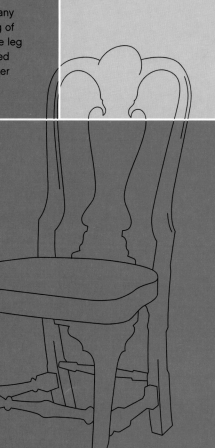

Queen Anne Side Chair
Period: 1725–1750

The restrained and graceful early phase of the Rococo style is named for England's Queen Anne, who died in 1714. This style introduced the cabriole leg to English and American furniture design. The ends of the yoke-shape top rail turn down to form the stiles; the vase-shape splat is solid rather than pierced with carving. Chairs may have slipper feet or ball-and-claw feet. The style overlaps both the earlier William and Mary and the later Chippendale styles.

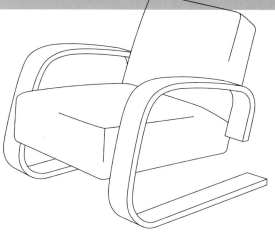

Lounge Chair **Designer:** Alvar Aalto
Date of design: 1935–1936

Bent-plywood legs that recall sled runners curve up to form the arms, creating a squared-C profile. The original design, made in Finland by Artek, has a foam-filled seat and back covered with a zebra print.

Sofas and love seats

Backless couches, the ancestor of modern sofas, appear on Greek pottery from the 8th century B.C.E. The Romans adopted them as daytime recliners and nighttime beds, but the furniture form began to flower when 18th-century French cabinetmakers went to work. Comfy sofas and love seats are now the cornerstones of family room and living room decorating and are far plumper and more padded than antique examples.

Empire Sofa Period: 1815–1840 This scroll-end or scroll-arm sofa shape, with its strongly curving arms and legs, was based on a Roman couch. The Empire style originated in Paris and reflected Emperor Napoleon's ambition to identify himself with great conquerors of the past. The style influenced furniture design all over Europe. Expensive pieces feature high-relief carving and gilded brass or bronze ornaments on arms and legs. Less expensive, machine-made pieces dispensed with the ornaments and emphasized strong, bold lines.

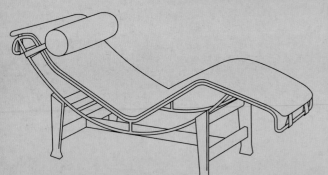

Chaise Longue B306
Designer: C. Perriand, P. Jeanneret, and Le Corbusier
Period: 1928
One of the best known pieces by this design team, the chaise updates the Roman notion of a recliner with ergonomics and a form inspired by Thonet's bentwood rocker of 1880.

Camelback Sofa
Period: 1750–1780
The arched shape of the back features the undulating rococo curves favored for mantels and furnishings of the 18th century. Both Queen Anne and Chippendale examples have cabriole legs and the Chinese-inspired ball-and-claw feet.

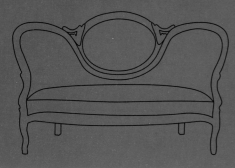

Rococo Revival Sofa
Period: 1840–1880

Although much more elaborately carved and molded frames were made, simpler frames like this were widely produced, usually as part of an entire suite of parlor furniture. Two of the best-known manufacturers of elaborately carved Rococo Revival furnishings were John Henry Belter and J. and J. W. Meeks, both of New York.

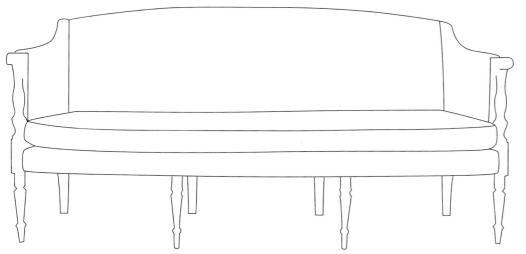

Federal Square-Back Sofa **Period:** 1780–1810
Federal style is the American interpretation of the neoclassic Sheraton and Hepplewhite styles that flourished in England in the 1760s. A sofa similar to this one appeared in Thomas Sheraton's pattern book, *The Cabinet-Maker and Upholsterer's Drawing Book* (1793). American cabinetmakers mixed Sheraton and Hepplewhite elements freely. Sofas and chairs featured slender, straight legs, a rectilinear profile, and delicate inlay rather than carving for decoration.

Sofa Compact
Designer: Charles and Ray Eames
Date of design: 1954
Designed for small suburban spaces of the 1950s, this sofa was the last low-cost piece of furniture that Charles and Ray Eames designed. It was inspired by a built-in sofa in their California home. The back folds down flat over the seat so the sofa is easier to ship. A steel frame with chrome-plated legs supports the foam-cushion seat and back. This piece has been in continuous production since 1954.

Marshmallow Sofa **Designer: George Nelson** Date of design: 1956
Anticipating Pop art in its defiantly unconventional form and bold color, the Marshmallow sofa was ahead of its time: Only a few hundred were made during the 10 years it was originally in production at Herman Miller, but now it's back, with a choice of fabrics or leather.

Heywood-Wakefield Love Seat (Aristocraft Line)
Designer: W. Joseph Carr
Date of design: 1954
Unlike many of the chubby, overstuffed upholstered pieces made by Heywood-Wakefield, the seating pieces in the Aristocraft line feature streamlined wooden arms and exposed legs that create a more lightweight look.

tables

In the 18th century, increasing attention to comfort resulted in a greater variety of table forms designed to serve specific functions. For much of the 19th century, round or oval tables intended to stand in front of sofas were between 27 and 32 inches tall. But beginning in the late 1800s, Moorish and Chinese interiors became fashionable and introduced the idea of placing low trays in front of seating. These low tray tables paved the way for the 20th-century coffee table.

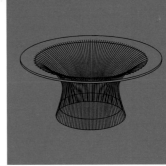

No. 3714 Coffee Table
Designer: Warren Platner
Date of design: 1966
The table is part of a collection that manufacturer Knoll International describes as "practical sculpture." Hundreds of steel wires are welded to circular frames, using a process Platner himself invented.

Revolving-Top Cocktail Table
Designer: Heywood-Wakefield
Date of production: 1956–1961
Arching steam-bent solid birch legs give an aerodynamic look to tables produced by Heywood-Wakefield in the 1950s. The revolving top accommodated casual entertaining.

Barcelona Table
Designer: Mies van der Rohe
Date of design: 1930
Properly named the Tugendhat table, after the residence for which it was designed, this piece consists of clear glass resting on an X-shape brace of stainless steel. The misnomer occurred when the table was brought back into production in 1948.

Model 2633
Designer: Pietro Chiesa
Date of design: 1937
This elegantly simple table of shaped ¾-inch clear crystal glass was designed by the multitalented art director of Fontana Arte, an Italian lighting and furniture manufacturer. It has inspired similar tables in Lucite.

Pedestal Table
Designer: Eero Saarinen **Date of design:** 1956
Aiming to clean up the forest of legs that clutters many rooms, Saarinen created this gravity-defying design. The top—laminate, marble, or granite—rests on a slender stem of molded cast aluminum. Available in round and oval versions, the tables come three sizes: dining, coffee, and side tables.

Coffee Table
Designer: Charles and Ray Eames
Date of design: 1946
Designed to accompany the couple's molded-plywood chairs, this coffee table is shaped like a large plywood dinner plate resting on bent-plywood legs. Production stopped in 1957 but has been resumed.

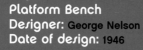

Platform Bench
Designer: George Nelson
Date of design: 1946

As design director of Herman Miller, Nelson aimed for versatility. This wooden bench, offered in six lengths and two finishes (natural with ebonized base or entirely ebonized), could also be a table, a plant stand, or a cabinet base.

Noguchi Coffee Table
Designer: Isamu Noguchi
Date of design: 1944

The flowing shapes and pure form of this coffee table hint at the influence of Noguchi's mentor, sculptor Constantin Brancusi. Noguchi first modeled the design for this table in plastic; he later created the prototype, using solid walnut for the interlocking legs, which form a tripod base for the thick glass top. Herman Miller manufactured the table from 1947 until 1972, then reintroduced it in 1984.

Queen Anne Tea Table
Period: 1730–1760

Tea tables originated in Boston and became popular elsewhere in the North American colonies. Clean lines, a rectangular top (often with a raised molded edge), and elegant cabriole legs with pad or slipper feet characterized pieces made in New England.

Federal Side Table
Period: 1795–1810

Semicircular, or demilune, tables were used in dining rooms as serving tables or extensions of the dining table; in parlors they were pushed against the wall as pier tables.

Pembroke Table **Period:** 1780–1820
Said to be named for the Welsh Countess of Pembroke who first ordered such a table, this 27-inch-tall table has two drop leaves. The tapered legs and oval drawer pull indicate Hepplewhite style. Tables were also made in the Chippendale style.

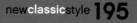

Chippendale Tilt-Top Tea Table Period: 1760–1770s

Philadelphia cabinetmakers elaborated the simple tea table into this complex (and slightly taller) form, with a round top resting on a "birdcage" support that allowed the top to rotate and to tilt upright so the table could be stowed flat against the wall. The baluster-shape base is supported by three cabriole legs that, in typical Chippendale style, end in ball-and-claw feet. New York cabinetmakers often decorated the knees of the cabriole legs with deeply cut carving.

Stool Model No. 60 Designer: Alvar Aalto Date of design: 1932–1933

Crafted of bent laminated birch, this stool doubles as a side table and is stackable. It captures flexible function distilled to its simplest form, an enduring interest for Aalto.

Colonial Revival Drop-Leaf Table Period: 1920–1935

Manufacturers used machine production to mimic 17th-century block-and-turned legs and stretchers and to create the drop-leaf top; they also scaled down pieces to suit smaller homes.

Empire Card Table Period: 1830–1850

Dolphin-shape supports supply the curvilinear silhouette that characterizes the Empire style. Casters, a 19th-century innovation, made it easy to move tables and chairs into different arrangements as needed.

Ellipse Table Designer: Charles and Ray Eames Date of design: 1950

Shaped like a surfboard and mounted on wire-strut bases, this table is made of seven-ply Baltic birch plywood with a white or black laminate top. At a daunting 89 inches in length, the table requires a spacious living room—or office reception area. Much of the modern furniture designed in the 1950s was intended for commercial rather than residential use.

Chests, cupboards, desks

Called case goods by the furniture industry, chests, cupboards, desks, and sideboards make a strong statement in a room and have a big impact on its design personality. Use the clean lines of a Sheraton sideboard, an Asian chest, or an Eames storage unit to anchor a room; add seating with similarly spare lines for a fresh, uncluttered look. Or reverse the mix and start with an ornate 18th- or 19th-century-style piece and accent it with the smooth, organic lines of Scandinavian modern seating.

Chippendale Secretary
Period: 1755–1780

Made in two sections, the secretary combined a slant-top desk with a cupboard top. The scrolled bonnet top with finials carried over from the Queen Anne style. Both flat and block-front models were available.

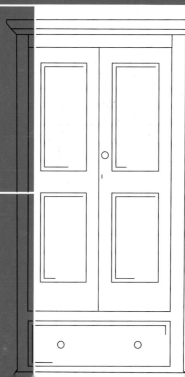

M320 Kneehole Desk
Designer: Heywood-Wakefield
Date of production: 1950–1965

The streamlined look of the 1930s lingers in the steam-bent drawer fronts that curve smoothly toward the center opening. The slim half-elliptical handles placed asymmetrically toward the inner edge reinforce the curve. Two of the left drawer fronts disguise a deep file drawer.

Sheraton Sideboard
Period: 1795–1820

Sideboards became standard dining room furniture in the second half of the 18th century. Inlaid veneers rather than carving provided the decoration. These graceful storage pieces can work equally well in a living room or hall.

Paneled Wardrobe
Period: 1790–1870

Wardrobes were essential furniture before the era of built-in closets. The top portion had pegs for hanging clothes or shelves for stacking folded items. Paneled doors, a plinthlike base, and a simple crown molding reflect the influence of neoclassical style. Paneled doors are a mark of quality, requiring more skill to craft than flat doors.

Bachelor's Chest
Period: 1695–1714

This English Queen Anne chest was a popular innovation of the period. Four rows of drawers rest on a base with bracket feet. The top folds out to rest on two arms that slide out from beside the top drawers. Low chests of drawers appeared in America in the late 1700s but were lower and longer than this English chest. The bat-wing drawer pulls are characteristic of both Queen Anne and Chippendale styles.

Victorian China Cabinet
Period: 1890–1920

The Victorians developed specialized pieces to showcase their knickknacks. Oak is the most common material; curved sides were an innovation made possible by newly available and inexpensive plate glass.

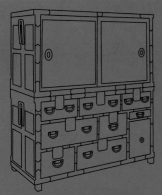

Marriage Chest **Period:** 18th century

Made in Korea, this plain wooden chest with metal pulls and trim reflects Japanese and Korean traditions, in which simplicity and function are paramount. Marco Polo may have introduced this furniture form to Europe in the 13th century, when he took home plain wooden cabinets and chests of drawers made in China.

French Armoire
Period: Late 18th century

An undulating crown gives French country armoires a graceful profile. The scrolled carving on the door panels rises toward the center, emphasizing the line. Inspired by elements of earlier French styles, from Louis XIII to Louis XVI, such armoires served in turn as sources of inspiration for revival styles in the 19th and 20th centuries.

Storage Unit
Designer: Charles and Ray Eames
Date of design: 1951

Using industrial materials—perforated aluminum, dimpled plywood, painted hardboard panels, and a steel frame—the Eameses created a modular storage unit intended for home rather than office use. Originally the paint colors were clear primaries, white, and black; Herman Miller now offers the unit in five configurations and two color choices.

Louis XV Commode
Designer: Garnier
Period: 1723–1774

This small serpentine-front chest bulges in a gracefully sinuous curve that repeats in the contours of the legs. Marquetry embellishes the highly polished surfaces, and gilded bronze mounts form the handles and feet and decorate the corners, keyholes, and apron.

Blockfront Kneehole Desk **Period:** 1765–1780

Blockfront construction (the division of the piece into two protruding sections and one recessed section) appears on secretaries, chests of drawers, and bureau tables made in New England in the mid-18th century. The recessed portion seems too narrow for a seated adult, but a plate in Thomas Chippendale's 1762 edition of *The Gentleman and Cabinet-Maker's Director* shows "buroe dressing tables" with similar recessed centers. The strongly carved shells and blockfront treatment are particularly associated with Newport, Rhode Island, cabinetmakers.

who's who in furniture design

Florence Knoll

Until the 17th century, cabinetmakers, joiners, and wood-carvers labored in anonymity, and furniture designs were passed down through guilds. In the 17th century, French and Dutch designers began to publish pattern books that helped spread a vocabulary of design and ornament throughout Europe. Cabinetmakers drew freely on these books for motifs and elements they could apply to furnishings of all types. Some of the names most familiar to Americans are those of the 18th-century Englishmen Thomas Chippendale, George Hepplewhite, and Thomas Sheraton, cabinetmakers whose pattern books disseminated furniture styles that became associated with their names. Like the 17th-century pattern books, the new volumes compiled motifs from various sources and offered dozens of variations on themes that individual cabinetmakers could copy or adapt as they saw fit.

In the 20th century, furniture design acquired new status as it became the business of professional architects, industrial designers, and interior designers. You don't need to know the name of the designer to know that a graceful bent-plywood chair would look perfect in your living room—but if you know that the chair you want is by Alvar Aalto, you'll be better able to track one down, whether vintage or new.

Here's a quick look at some of the names you're likely to encounter in any discussion of furniture classics.

George Nelson

Ludwig Mies van der Rohe

Isamu Noguchi

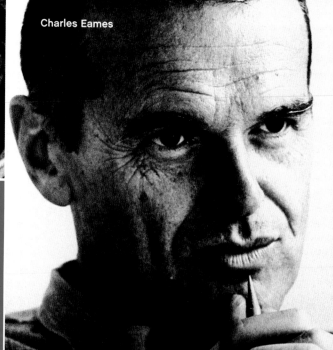

Charles Eames

Hugo Alvar Henrik Aalto
(1898–1976)

One of Finland's most influential architects, Alvar Aalto (pronounced olvar al'to) began experimenting with molding native blond birch plywood to make furniture in 1929. He introduced his first pieces in 1931, and in 1935 he founded Artek, a furniture design company, with his wife, architect Aino Marsio-Aalto, and a couple of backers. One of his major innovations was applying the architectural principle of the cantilever to build a bent-plywood chair. Even after its introduction and the patenting of the process in 1935, he continued to experiment and refine the chair, settling on webbing instead of upholstery because of its greater resilience. His work gained international acclaim when it appeared at the Paris Exhibition in 1937 and the New York World's Fair in 1939. Unlike the tubular-steel pieces of other modernists, Aalto's shaped wood furniture communicated warmth and seemed to humanize modern buildings. His architectural designs are noted for their sensitivity to the site, sun and lighting, and acoustics. Like other modernists, Aalto was interested in mass production and worked to devise standard parts that could be adapted to multiple uses. In addition to buildings and furniture, he designed glassware and jewelry and collaborated with Aino on interior designs.

Mario Bellini (1935–)

A prolific and versatile Italian designer, Bellini studied at the Polytechnic of Milan, graduating in 1959. In 1961 he became design director for the department store chain La Rinascente; in 1963 he joined Olivetti, where he began by designing computer terminals, teleprinters, and typewriters. In addition to serving as design consultant for Olivetti, Bellini is also research and design consultant for Renault and has created products for B&B Italia, Cassina, Vitra (office furnishings), Yamaha, Artemide, Fiat, and Lancia. His designs, which bring together marketability, mass production, and "good Italian design," were the subject of a one-man show at the Museum of Modern Art in 1987. Some of his work is part of the permanent collection there. Bellini also practices architecture.

John Henry Belter (1804–1863)

Born in Germany, Belter immigrated to New York in 1844 and opened a furniture-making shop. His experiments with laminating and steam-bending rosewood yielded a strong product that could be carved and pierced in intricate designs. He attempted to patent his processes, but his methods were widely imitated, probably spread in part by journeymen carvers and craftsmen who moved from shop to shop. Belter employed German carvers who immigrated at the same time he did; their naturalistic carving style produced the elaborate leaves, grapes, vines, and bouquets for which American Rococo Revival furniture is known.

Harry Bertoia (1915–1978)

Born in Italy, Bertoia came to America as a teenager with his family. He attended the influential Cranbrook Academy of Art on a teaching scholarship from 1937 to 1939, then opened a metalworking studio there and taught from 1939 to 1943. At Cranbrook, he met Charles and Ray Eames and Eero Saarinen and in 1943 moved to California to work with them at Evans Products Company. The Eameses and Saarinen were experimenting with molding plywood at this time. Bertoia left in 1946 and accepted an offer from another Cranbrook graduate, Florence Knoll, to design at her studio in Pennsylvania. Working in that atmosphere of artistic freedom, he devised his famous wire chairs, part of a complete set of steel-mesh furniture that expressed his overriding interest in sculpture. Although the chairs captured the feeling of modernity, they actually had to be made by hand because no mass production technology was available. Furniture manufacturer Herman Miller thought the design looked too much like an Eames design and took Knoll International to court. Herman Miller won and gave Knoll a license to produce the chairs. Bertoia remained as a consultant to Knoll into the 1970s but focused most of his energy on metal sculpture.

Marcel Breuer (1902–1981)

Born in Hungary, Breuer (pronounced broyer) created some of the most influential furniture to come out of the Bauhaus. He studied at the school from 1920 to 1924 and became master of the workshop there for a year before leaving to open an architectural practice in Berlin. His experiments with tubular steel resulted in what is now known as the Wassily chair, a Cubist construction of bent steel with canvas panels for seat and back (1925). He continued to tweak and improve the design, and furniture manufacturer Thonet offered a variation in its 1930 catalog. Breuer's design (and a cantilevered chair designed by Mart Stam) encouraged other modernist architects to begin working with tubular steel. Although his Cesca chair, named after his daughter, debuted after Mart Stam's design, it refined the concept and became the most successful of the cantilevered chairs, inspiring many imitations. Breuer left Germany to escape Nazi persecution, settling in London in 1931, where he worked as an architect and then as controller of design at Isokon. In 1937, he moved to the United States and joined Walter Gropius on the teaching staff at Harvard University. Breuer also shared an architectural practice with Gropius during that time. He headed his own firm from 1946 to 1976.

Thomas Chippendale
(1718–1779)

An English cabinetmaker, Chippendale published *The Gentleman and Cabinet-Maker's Director* in 1754 and updated editions in 1755 and 1762. Hundreds of popular motifs, including rococo, Chinese, and Gothic elements, were illustrated, along with examples of ways to use them. His pattern books were responsible for the new style of decorating chair splats and highboys with pierced carving. Chippendale also introduced the straight, or Marlborough, leg as an updated replacement for the cabriole leg, but American cabinetmakers continued to prefer the curved leg and ball-and-claw foot long after the form had been abandoned in England.

Donald Deskey (1894–1989)

Deskey studied architecure at the University of California, but his studies were interrupted by World War I. In 1923, he moved to Paris, where he married, studied painting, and visited the Paris Exhibition in 1925. There, he saw the elegant and luxurious style of furnishings and accessories that became known as Art Deco; he also saw some of the first modernist furnishings and interiors. Returning to New York City, he started his own company designing furniture, interiors, and products ranging from pianos, clocks, and slot machines to industrial materials and textiles. Deskey's work was modernist in feeling and materials, relying on chrome, aluminum, and Bakelite and embracing clean-lined, unornamented forms; but he freely incorporated Art Deco elements if a project (such as the interiors of Radio City Music Hall, 1932–1933) seemed to warrant it.

Charles Eames (1907–1978)
Ray Eames (1912–1989)

Charles was born in St. Louis and attended the Cranbrook Academy of Art on a fellowship beginning in 1936. He was teaching there as head of the industrial design department when Ray Kaiser (born Bernice Alexandra Kaiser) came to take weaving classes. Ray was a Californian and had studied painting with Hans Hofmann in New York City (1933-1939). She exhibited with the first American Abstract Artists' group show in 1937. She and Charles married in 1941 and began collaborating almost immediately. During World War II, the United States Navy hired them to design stackable plywood splints and litters; this encouraged their experiments with molding plywood in three dimensions, which continued after the war. Earlier, in 1940, Charles had collaborated with Cranbrook classmate Eero Saarinen to produce the winning design for the "Organic Design in Home Furnishings" competition held by the Museum of Modern Art (MoMA) in New York. In 1946, MoMA gave Charles a one-man show, and in 1948 he won second prize in the museum competition for low-cost furniture design; the winning entries were mass-producible molded fiberglass chairs that he and Ray designed. As a team, they worked with Herman Miller through the 1950s and 1960s, creating some of the most influential modern furniture designs in America (many for commercial rather than residential use). Some pieces could not be produced until decades later, when appropriate technology was developed. In the 1970s, until Charles's death in 1978, the Eameses applied their talents to filmmaking, toys, photography, and exhibition design.

Norman Bel Geddes (1893–1958)

Bel Geddes (ged'eez) briefly attended the Cleveland Institute of Art and the Chicago Institute of Art, but left school to work as a set designer for the Metropolitan Opera in 1918. While working in stage design, he introduced innovative uses of lighting. In 1927 Bel Geddes began working as an industrial designer and became a major proponent of streamlining as an approach to shaping form for better function. His projects ranged from individual products (such as a radio cabinet for Philco, scales for the Toledo Scale Company, and an automobile) to theaters and an elaborate Futurama exhibit for General Motors at the 1939 New York World's Fair. His book *Horizons*, published in 1932, presented imaginative and futuristic designs for cars, transoceanic airplanes, and buildings.

Eileen Gray (1878–1976)

Born in Ireland, Gray studied at London's Slade School of Art. In 1902, she went to France and studied drawing at two popular academies for foreign students, the Académies Colarossi and Julian. Before World War I, she began designing lacquer furniture; after 1919, she designed interiors as well as modernist furniture, including tubular-steel pieces. After 1926 she took on architectural projects. Like other modernists, Gray was interested in multifunctional pieces that could morph into different forms— a desk into a cabinet, a chair into a stepladder.

Walter Gropius (1883–1969)

Born in Berlin, Gropius worked in the office of influential architect Peter Behrens from 1908 to 1910 before opening his own office. In 1919 he was appointed director of a trade school in Weimar, which he merged with another school to form Staatliches Bauhaus. The school moved to Dessau in 1925, and Gropius continued as director until 1928. Through his direction of the Bauhaus, Gropius influenced the formation of an entire generation of modernists; the guiding principle at the school was the unity of all the arts, with architecture as "the mother of the arts." His design (in collaboration with Adolf Meyer) of the Fagus Shoe Factory in Germany (1911–1916) broke new ground in its use of the curtain wall—expanses of glass in place of solid walls. His designs for the Bauhaus buildings expressed a new concept of architectural space, with flat roofs, long horizontal planes of white walls, and unbroken ribbons of windows creating light-filled, open interiors. In 1934 Gropius left for London and became head of design at Isokon. In 1937 he came to the United States, where he taught architecture at Harvard University from 1937 until 1952.

George Hepplewhite (died 1786)

An English cabinetmaker, Hepplewhite compiled furniture designs and motifs into a pattern book that his wife published in 1788 after his death. *Cabinet Maker and Upholsterer's Guide* adapted the neoclassicism of Scottish architect Robert Adam to elegant furniture forms. Hepplewhite popularized shield-shape or lyre-shape chair backs, tapered and reeded legs, and the use of inlaid veneer to embellish surfaces.

Arne Jacobsen (1902–1971)

One of the best-known Danish architects, Arne Jacobsen (pronounced arn yahkopsn) trained as a mason before studying architecture at the Royal Academy of Arts in Copenhagen, Denmark. In 1929, his entry in a contest for the House of the Future was a circular building with a helicopter landing pad on the roof. He and a partner also designed all the furniture, textiles, and color choices, foreshadowing his preferred method of working: designing every aspect of a project, from the building to the furnishings and details. In 1930 he founded his own architectural practice, which he headed until his death. His famous Ant chair, molded plywood on metal legs, evolved from a design for a child's school chair. His best-known projects include St. Catherine's College, Oxford, and the SAS or Royal Hotel, Copenhagen. His work wasn't immediately popular—the 1956 SAS Hotel was voted the ugliest building in the city. His Swan and Egg chairs, created for the hotel, were both sculptural and functional, designed to accommodate a variety of sitting positions. Nearly two decades later, Jacobsen's vision was still perceived as futuristic: The flatware designed for the hotel was used in the film *2001: A Space Odyssey*.

Finn Juhl (1912–1989)

A Danish architect, Finn Juhl (pronounced yule) graduated from the Royal Academy of Arts in Copenhagen in 1934. From 1935 to 1945 he worked as an architect in an established office, then opened his own practice in 1945, specializing in furniture and interior design. His designs won five gold medals at Milan Triennale exhibitions. Like other

Scandinavians, he blended Danish handcrafting traditions with machine production, achieving a sculptural effect with beautifully finished walnut and distinctive "floating" seats and backs. Inspired by tribal art and abstract organic sculpture, his designs in the 1940s helped revitalize Danish furniture making. Early chairs, such as the Chieftain chair (1949), were produced in small quantities for the Copenhagen Cabinetmakers Guild shows. Most were later reissued and mass-produced. In 1951 Juhl designed 24 pieces for furniture manufacturer Baker in Grand Rapids, Michigan, aimed at a younger market. His exhibits of Danish applied arts at international exhibitions in the 1960s helped popularize Danish modern in America and Europe.

Florence (Schust) Knoll (1917–)

An American architect trained at the Cranbrook Academy of Art as well as in London and at the Illinois Institute of Technology (where she studied under Mies van der Rohe), Florence Knoll was thoroughly grounded in modernist theory and practice. Before marrying Hans Knoll in 1946, she worked in the Cambridge, Massachusetts, offices of Walter Gropius and Marcel Breuer. Hans, a German, moved to America in 1938 to start a furniture company. He and Florence renamed the company Knoll Associates in 1946 and focused on modern design, adhering to the Bauhaus philosophy of making products that "represented design excellence, technological innovation and mass production." They also adopted a policy of crediting individual designers and

paying them royalties. When Florence obtained the rights to manufacture Mies's Barcelona series, the company became a leader in the International style in America. To ensure ready access to suitable fabrics, they started their own textiles division. Florence Knoll also designed furniture and exhibited at the "Good Design" shows held by the Museum of Modern Art (MoMA).

Erwine and Estelle Laverne (1909– and 1915–1998)

The Lavernes studied painting with Hans Hofmann at the Art Students League in New York City. As entrepreneurs, they founded a manufacturing and retailing company in 1938 called Laverne Originals, which produced fabrics and wallcoverings created by a team of designers. In the late 1950s the couple began designing furniture themselves, introducing the Invisible Group in 1957. The chairs, clear molded Perspex on slender pedestal bases, were inspired by Saarinen's Tulip series and anticipated Pop furniture of the 1960s. This series was followed by the Lotus, a curvaceous black molded fiberglass chair with a curvy metal base and cutout back, and their own Tulip chair, which looked like petals opening. The company showroom was a radical departure from custom, a nearly empty space that felt and functioned like an art gallery.

Le Corbusier (1887–1965)

Swiss architect Charles-Edouard Jeanneret took his maternal grandmother's family name, Le Corbusier (korbuzyay), to use as a pseudonym for his contributions to

the magazine *L'Esprit Nouveau*, which he published with fellow artist Amedée Ozenfant from 1920 to 1925. A dedicated painter, Le Corbusier is best known for helping define the principles of the International style. He wrote prolifically, promoting the idea that buildings are machines for performing certain functions. (His description of a house as a "machine for living" would give conservative critics ammunition for blasting the perceived inhuman coldness of modernism.) He argued that just as engineers must understand the technical requirements of an airplane to create a machine for flying, so architects must understand the technical requirements of a house to design a building that functions well for living. In 1927, Charlotte Perriand, an interior designer and furniture designer, joined him and his cousin Pierre Jeanneret in their Paris office, and the three collaborated on the furniture designs that have become icons of modernism. The Chaise Longue and the Confort (Petit and Grand versions), shown at the 1928 Salon des Artistes Decorateurs, were intended for mass production but were too expensive. The chaise, based on a bentwood rocker by Thonet, was originally manufactured by Thonet and reintroduced in 1965 by Cassina. The Grand Confort, designed for comfortable reading or conversation, reinterpreted the French bergère but turned it inside out, exposing the skeletal structure. Its Cubist form reflected the influence of Josef Hoffmann's 1910 Kubus chair.

Raymond Loewy (1893–1986)

A prolific industrial designer, Loewy was born in France and moved to the United States in 1919 to pursue graphic design. Creating window displays for Macy's and Saks Fifth Avenue encouraged him to establish his own design firm in 1930. Eventually he had offices in England and France as well. As a marketer, Loewy understood and exploited the power of image to help sell products. Making extensive use of teardrop and streamlined shapes, he helped create the look of early modernism in America. His projects ranged from the design of the Lucky Strike cigarette package to the iconic Coca-Cola bottle. Loewy also designed locomotive engines, cars, and refrigerators. In the late 1960s NASA hired him to design the interior of the Skylab space station.

Charles Rennie Mackintosh (1868–1928)

Born in Glasgow, Scotland, Mackintosh trained as an architect in established architectural firms. He began designing furniture in 1896. For his best-known commission (a chain of tearooms), he applied a cohesive artistic vision to the project, designing (with his wife, Margaret Macdonald) interiors, furniture, carpets, wall treatments, and all of the details, including the cutlery and glassware. Initially Mackintosh worked in an organic, Art Nouveau style, but his austere, strongly vertical furniture, which drew no inspiration from past models or traditional styles, appealed to the early modernists. His approach to architecture—as a response to the

requirements of the space rather than decoration of a structure—also represented an innovation.

Bruno Mathsson (1907–1988)

Swedish furniture designer and architect Mathsson trained in his father's cabinetmaking workshop. In 1930 he began applying his knowledge of the character and properties of wood to new technology to design lightweight, easy-to-assemble furnishings made of bent laminated wood. Exhibitions of his organic, ergonomic furnishings in Paris (1937), the Museum of Modern Art (1939), and San Francisco (1939) helped bring international attention to modern Swedish furniture design. From 1945 to 1958 he also practiced architecture, designing schoolrooms and innovative glass houses.

Ludwig Mies van der Rohe (1886–1969)

Born in Aachen, Germany, and trained as a builder, Mies van der Rohe absorbed a respect for craftsmanship from his father, who was a master mason. Mies moved to Berlin in 1905 to study architecture under Bruno Paul, then joined Peter Behrens's firm in 1908. In 1929, Mies received a last-minute commission to design the German Pavilion for the Barcelona International Exhibition. A temporary structure, the pavilion showcased his famous "less is more" approach to architecture: It was a minimalist composition of planes and lines with freestanding interior walls. The chairs, stools, and tables he designed for the pavilion, and for the Tugendhat house in Czechoslovakia the

following year, have become modern classics. In 1931 furniture maker Thonet-Mundus bought exclusive marketing rights to 15 chair designs (some of which can be credited to Mies's associate Lilly Reich). Mies was the last director of the Bauhaus and closed the school in 1933 in response to pressure from the Nazis. In 1938, he moved to the United States, where he taught architecture at the Illinois Institute of Technology in Chicago. His best-known buildings in America include the Seagram Building in New York City, designed with Philip Johnson (1958), and the Farnsworth House in Illinois.

William Morris (1834–1896)

The founder of the English Arts and Crafts Movement, Morris deplored the rise of machine production and its impact on society. He blamed the machine for degrading public taste with cheap, poor-quality goods and thoughtlessly eclectic art and architecture. A poet, painter, designer of textiles and wallpaper, and social reformer, he advocated a return to the handcrafting traditions of the Middle Ages as a way of solving 19th-century social ills. Although his romantic medievalism was as much an academic revival as the eclecticism he criticized, his insistence on taste and quality of craftsmanship inspired the next generation of designers to reconcile mass production with high standards of design.

George Nelson (1908–1986)

Best known to collectors of midcentury modern furniture as the design director of Herman Miller and the creator of multifunctional

pieces such as the Platform Bench of 1947, George Nelson was first a classically trained architect. After graduating from Yale University with a degree in architecture in 1931, he studied in Rome at the American Academy, where he won the Prix de Rome for architecture. As editor of *Architectural Forum* from 1935 to 1944, he won a reputation as a design theorist and architecture critic. In 1946 he joined Herman Miller as design director; through his commissions from other designers as well as his own work, he had a major impact on the development of modern furniture design in America. Nelson's design legacy includes revolutionary storage and office systems and multifunctional furniture for offices and homes, as well as 1950s icons such as asterisk-shape numberless clocks, the Marshmallow sofa, and the Coconut chair. Nelson is also credited with the idea of the shopping mall.

Isamu Noguchi (1904–1988)

American-born Isamu Noguchi (pronounced samoo nogooch) lived in Japan from age 2 to 14. In 1918 he returned to America to attend school and studied briefly with an academic realist sculptor. On a fellowship in Paris, he met Constantin Brancusi and worked as his assistant for six months. The exposure to Cubists, Constructivists, and other avant-garde artists moved him away from academic realism toward his own abstract, organic style. Exceptionally prolific and creative, Noguchi studied Chinese brush painting, Japanese ceramics, and Japanese garden design; he channeled these and other influences into projects as diverse as sets for modern dancer Martha Graham; fountains, parks, playgrounds, and gardens; and furniture and lighting, which he approached as useful sculpture. He began creating Akari lamps from paper and bamboo in 1951 and continued designing them the rest of his life. "Akari," a name he made up, is Japanese for "light as illumination" and also conveys the idea of lightness in terms of weight. His iconic coffee table was first modeled in plastic at the request of designer and architect T.H. Robsjohn-Gibbings; later Noguchi saw a variation published as a Robsjohn-Gibbings design. He protested, and Robsjohn-Gibbings's response, that anyone could make a three-legged table, prompted Noguchi to produce a modified version of his original design, which illustrated an article written by George Nelson entitled "How to Make a Table." Herman Miller, Inc., bought the rights to manufacture the table and produced it from 1947 to 1973, then resumed production in 1984.

Verner Panton (1926–1998)
Trained at the Royal Danish Academy of Fine Arts in Copenhagen, Panton (pronounced penton) worked in Arne Jacobsen's architectural firm for a time, then established his own design office in 1955. Unlike Jacobsen, Panton broke with Danish tradition, embracing new materials and technologies and redefining how chairs should function and what they should look like. His Cone chair completely dispenses with conventional shape, consisting of sheet metal bent into a geometric figure and covered with upholstery.

In 1960 he designed the first single-form injection-molded plastic chair, the stackable Panton chair. A similar S chair in plywood debuted in 1966, produced by Thonet. Panton also designed textiles as well as lighting that was unconventional and playful.

Pierre Paulin (1927–)
Paulin (po lanh), a French artist, studied stone carving and clay modeling, then began designing furniture for Thonet in 1954 and for Artifort in 1958. Described as both sculptural and functional, his furniture designs suggest organic, anthropomorphic inspiration, even though he assigned them numbers instead of names to avoid any "lyrical" effect. His notable commissions include refurbishing the Louvre in 1968 and designing furniture for the office of President François Mitterrand at the Elysee Palace in 1983.

Charlotte Perriand (1903–1999)
Born in Paris, Perriand (per-ee-awn) studied at the Ecole de Lunin Centrale des Arts Decoratifs in Paris. Her design for a "bar in the garret" at the Salon d'Automne in 1927 caught the attention of Le Corbusier, who then invited her to join his office. She is now credited with primary responsibility for most of the furniture that came from Le Corbusier's studio. After leaving the firm in 1937, Perriand pursued architectural projects that included a ski resort, the tea area for the UNESCO garden in Paris, prefabricated aluminum buildings, and the interiors and furnishings for United Nations conference rooms in Geneva. As a member of associations connected to or

sponsored by the Communist Party, Perriand aimed to create quality furnishings for the lower and middle classes. Ironically, the iconic pieces released under Le Corbusier's name were too expensive for most consumers. Her furniture designs for Thonet were reissued by Cassina.

Warren Platner (1919–)
Born in Baltimore, Platner studied architecture at Cornell University, Ithaca, New York. His early work experience exposed him to some of the most influential figures in American design, including Raymond Loewy, I. M. Pei, and Eero Saarinen. While working in Saarinen's office, he participated in the design of Dulles International Airport and the repertory theater at Lincoln Center. Platner established his own firm in 1965. A grant from the Graham Foundation allowed him to work with the Knoll production team to design the Platner Collection, his major furniture collection. He created both the structure and production method for ottomans, tables, and chairs composed of hundreds of steel rods that had to be individually welded to circular frames. The cylindrical, organic shapes suggest enclosed space but at the same time are penetrable, creating a dialogue of solids and voids.

Gio Ponti (1891–1979))
Ponti graduated from the Polytechnic of Milan with a degree in architecture in 1921. His work went far beyond architecture, however, to touch many aspects of Italian cultural life and influenced architecture, design, and art

publishing around the world. One of the first Italian architects to embrace modernism, Ponti also insisted that decoration and ornament were not incompatible with modern design. His low-cost furniture, Domus Nova, 1927, was available through the influential department store La Rinascente. His best-known design, produced by Cassina from 1957 on, is the Superleggera, or Superlight, a slender ladder-back chair that can be lifted with one finger. Ponti started the magazine *Domus* in 1928 to raise awareness of design issues; in 1941 he began publishing *Stile*, which focused on art. His Pirelli Tower in Milan was the tallest building in Europe when it was completed in 1956.

Jens Risom (1916–)
Born in Denmark and trained there in Copenhagen, Jens Risom (pronounced yenz rhee som) came to America in 1939 and is considered one of the most influential American designers of postwar modern design. In 1939, he and Hans Knoll worked together on an exhibition for the New York World's Fair; that project won Risom an invitation to create the interior for the House of Ideas in Rockefeller Center, sponsored by *Collier's* magazine. Risom also produced 15 designs for Knoll's first catalog in 1942. Because of wartime rationing, the chairs, stools, and lounges were made from cedar (rather than laminated wood) and webbing. For the next 20 years Risom designed furniture for George Jensen, Richard Avedon, and other prominent clients, but he also produced cabinets for Levitt & Sons tract houses on Long Island, the

landmark postwar American experiment in low-cost suburban housing. In 1961 *Playboy* magazine profiled Risom, Charles Eames, and Harry Bertoia as designers who were "revolutionizing furniture in America." In the 1960s Risom turned his attention to office furniture. His statement that "good design means that anything which is good by itself will go with other things" anticipated the 21st-century openness to mixing classics from all design periods.

Gilbert Rohde (1894–1944)

An American and the son of a cabinetmaker, Rohde started out as an illustrator at a department store. After visiting the Paris Exhibition in 1925 he began designing modern furniture that was sold at the high-end department store Lord & Taylor. Like Donald Deskey, he adopted Bauhaus rationalism and industrial materials, but he didn't hesitate to borrow forms and ornamentation from Parisian Art Deco. In 1931 he signed an agreement with Heywood-Wakefield to design a line of modern furniture, the first ever produced on an assembly line and the first to include sectional and modular pieces that could be mixed and matched in a variety of combinations. At the same time, he began creating new designs for Herman Miller, Inc., in Grand Rapids, Michigan. These included complete living and dining room sets as well as multipurpose furniture (card tables that could be dining tables, settees that turned into beds) and modular office furniture. Rohde also served as the design director at Herman Miller for several years. To help persuade retailers to stock the modern pieces, Rohde invented the idea of a manufacturer's showroom, where sales representatives could come to see the furniture. His work appeared at the Machine Art show at the Museum of Modern Art in 1934 and the 1939 New York World's Fair. From 1939 to 1943 he headed the industrial design department at the New York University School of Architecture.

Eero Saarinen (1910–1961)

Born in Finland, Saarinen came to the United States at age 13. His mother was a weaver and photographer, and his father was the well-known architect Eliel Saarinen, one of the founders of the Cranbrook Academy of Art in Michigan. Eero studied in Paris in 1929 and received his degree in architecture from Yale University in 1934. He worked briefly with Norman Bel Geddes as a furniture designer but then joined his father's practice in Ann Arbor, Michigan, and taught at Cranbrook. There he met Charles Eames and formed a fruitful partnership; some of the first results were landmark furniture designs that were featured in the 1940 "Organic Design in Home Furnishings" exhibition at the Museum of Modern Art. Saarinen and the Eameses continued to work together during and after the war, experimenting with molded plywood. Saarinen went on to design for Knoll; Eames, for Herman Miller. In the late 1940s Saarinen produced the bent-plywood Grasshopper chair, as well as the Womb chair, which was engineered to allow the sitter to be comfortable in a variety of positions. In the 1950s Saarinen introduced his famous pedestal furniture series made of fiberglass and aluminum. As important as his furniture designs were to midcentury modernism, his architectural legacy was even greater, including such landmarks as the Jefferson National Expansion Memorial Arch in St. Louis, "Gateway to the West"; the TWA terminal at John F. Kennedy International Airport; and Dulles International Airport in Washington, D.C.

Thomas Sheraton (1751–1806)

An English cabinetmaker whose elegant furniture combined influences from French Louis XVI and Directoire styles, Sheraton published a two-volume pattern book, *The Cabinet-Maker and Upholsterer's Drawing Book*, between 1791 and 1793. The books changed English furniture design, promoting the neoclassic motifs and proportions introduced by architect Robert Adam. In America, cabinetmakers tended to borrow from both Sheraton and Hepplewhite and to blend these influences with a homegrown Federal style. The main difference between Sheraton and Hepplewhite was that Sheraton tended to prefer rectilinear designs while Hepplewhite made greater use of curves. Sheraton's typical motifs included lyres, slender urns, and latticework, as well as swags, cockleshells, and fan shapes.

Mart Stam (1899–1986)

A Dutch designer, Stam began as a draftsman for an architectural firm in Rotterdam in the Netherlands. In 1922, he moved to Berlin and studied urban planning at the Bauhaus. In 1924, he developed a cantilevered tubular-steel chair for his wife, using lengths of straight pipe and gas fitter's joints. Exhibited in 1926, the chair caused excitement in modernist circles because it represented a progressive application of modern materials and architectural principles to a traditional furniture form. Other designers, including Mies van der Rohe and Marcel Breuer, later produced their own cantilevered tubular-steel furniture. Stam taught architecture and design in Germany after World War II and was appointed director of the Advanced Institute of Art in Berlin in 1950.

Gustav Stickley (1858–1942)

A leader of the Arts and Crafts movement in America and originator of the Mission style in furnishings, Stickley learned woodworking from his father and chair making from his uncle. In 1898 he traveled to England, where he absorbed William Morris's design philosophy. Unlike Morris, however, Stickley was willing to use machinery and mass production as a means of manufacturing well-designed, well-made, affordable furniture. Stickley relied on plank construction to give the furniture its shape and appearance; mortise and tenon joints were left exposed. The rectilinear designs, absence of ornament, and unpretentious functionalism of the pieces represented a reaction to the florid decorativeness of Victorian furniture. Stickley himself described his furniture as "simple, durable, comfortable and fitted for the place it was to occupy and the work it had to do." He promoted the furniture, his philosophy, and designs for bungalows and other housing styles through his magazine *The Craftsman*.

Michael Thonet (1796–1871)

Born in Prussia, Thonet (pronounced tone-ay) pioneered new methods of mass-producing economical, stylish chairs for commercial use. Some of his bent-plywood designs were also adopted for residential use, but his research and experimentation were aimed at the high-volume market of hotels, cafes, and restaurants. He learned the traditional methods of cabinetmaking through the apprenticeship system. In 1819 he married and opened his own shop, and for 11 years he made furniture the traditional way, hand-carving the parts and joining the finished pieces. In 1830, searching for a faster, more economical alternative to carving, Thonet began experimenting with steam-bending wood into curved ornamental shapes. He also experimented with laminating wood veneers to construct furniture; previously veneers had been used as surface decoration only. Thonet worked to reduce chair designs to the fewest possible parts that could be combined into a wide variety of designs. Although most of his designs were traditional, the bentwood chair No. 14 and the bentwood rocking chair inspired modernist designers with their simplicity of form, utility, and combination of manufactured material (plywood) and mass production.

Hans Wegner (1914–)

A Danish designer, Wegner (pronounced weeneh) trained in both carpentry and architecture. He worked with Arne Jacobsen until 1943, then opened his own office. Wegner readily drew on historical precedents but simplified and distilled forms to their essence. His approach to design, he says, is "stripping the old chairs of their outer style and letting them appear in their pure construction." With fellow Danes Finn Juhl, Arne Jacobsen, and Verner Panton, Wegner helped develop the "organic functionalism" of Danish modern design. Until the 1960s, he usually collaborated with a cabinetmaker, Johannes Hansen, to execute his ideas. The Peacock Chair debuted in 1947 at the Cabinetmakers' Guild of Copenhagen and brought international attention to his work. Each year thereafter he produced a new design, including the Folding Chair of 1949 and the Round Chair of 1950. The Round Chair appeared on the cover of *Interiors* magazine in 1950 and was described as "the world's most beautiful chair."

Frank Lloyd Wright (1867–1959)

Probably the single best-known American architect, Wright did not consider himself a modernist of the Bauhaus school, but his early designs influenced some of the Bauhaus members. Wright worked with the Chicago firm Adler and Sullivan from 1887 to 1893, then opened his own practice. With few major commissions for public or commercial projects in the early years, he turned his attention to residential architecture as the means for working out his design philosophy. His Prairie Style architecture emphasized long, low horizontal lines unified by strong verticals; deep overhangs that embrace the outdoor area contiguous with the house; and a central core made up of the chimney and utilities, with living spaces flowing freely from the core. Wright's early houses and plans were published in Europe by 1910, where they impressed Walter Gropius, J. J. P. Oud, Piet Mondrian, and others. Wright moved on to explore Asian and Mayan architecture, which influenced his design for the Imperial Hotel in Tokyo. One of his most famous buildings, the Solomon R. Guggenheim Museum in New York City, has been described by art historian H. H. Arnason as "one of the great architectural spaces of the twentieth century."

Russel Wright (1904–1976)

Russel Wright was one of the first American industrial designers to have his name become synonymous with lines of consumer goods—in essence, to become a brand. Although he studied at the Art Academy in Cincinnati, the Art Students League in New York, and Princeton, he never finished college. He worked briefly with industrial designer Norman Bel Geddes. In 1934 Heywood-Wakefield hired Wright to design modern furniture, and in 1935 he contracted with Conant Ball to market his American Modern line of solid-wood furniture. With his wife, Mary, and another partner, Wright formed Russel Wright Associates in 1935 and designed dinnerware, glassware, table linens, furniture, art pottery, and more for a variety of manufacturers. The American Modern line of dinnerware debuted in 1939, manufactured by Steubenville Pottery Company. Wright's life and work were the subject of an exhibition at the Cooper-Hewitt Museum in New York City in 2002.

Eva Zeisel (1906–)

Born in Budapest, Hungary, Zeisel studied painting, then apprenticed to a ceramist. Her earliest work was rectilinear, but she soon adopted a more organic, tactile approach to materials and forms. In 1932, Zeisel went to work in Russia at what was one of the largest ceramics factories in the world. She became art director of the China and Glass Industry of the Russian Republic, but growing hostility toward foreigners in the late 1930s forced her to leave. She moved to England and then to the United States in 1938. In 1942, Castleton Company asked the Museum of Modern Art in New York to locate a ceramist who could design modern china. Zeisel was chosen, and her elegant, all-white, biomorphic Museum Series of 1946 was the result. Zeisel retired from mass-produced commercial design in the mid-1960s.

Resources

Check these websites and shops to find modern furniture and accessories, both vintage and new.

Manufacturers

Alessi
Italian manufacturers of contemporary tableware and accessories. Visit the website alessi.it to view the product line, read about the company's history, and find a local retailer.

Artek
Manufacturers of furniture and lighting by Alvar Aalto, Aino Aalto, and other Finnish designers. For more information on individual products, visit the website at artek.fi. Artek products are distributed in the U.S. by Herman Miller (see below).

B&B Italia
Contemporary Italian design. For B&B Italia store locations visit bebitalia.it online.

Cassina
Headquartered in Milan with a U.S. showroom at 155 East 56th Street, New York City. Call 212/245-2121 to find a local dealer. If you visit the website (cassina.it) be prepared for a leisurely aesthetic experience.

Herman Miller
Located in Zeeland, Michigan, manufacturers of Eames, Noguchi, Nelson designs. The company now distributes furniture by Alvar Aalto too. Call 800/646-4400 for a local dealer or visit the website hmhome.com

Knoll International
Modern classics can be ordered from knollshop.com. Or visit knoll.com to find local dealers. Also check office-furnishings suppliers for Knoll products.

Ligne Roset
Manufactures contemporary furniture, lighting, textiles, and accessories. Visit the website ligne-roset.com to view product lines and to find the nearest distributor.

Vitra
Vitra manufactures Eames designs under license from Herman Miller, introduced the Panton chairs in 1966, and manufactures products by contemporary designers such as Mario Bellini with Dieter Thiel, Philippe Starck, and Frank Gehry. Visit the website vitra.com to find local dealers.

Online Shopping

1950
Classic modern furniture, lighting, and accessories. 1950.com

Aalto.com
Designs by Alvar Aalto that are still in production can be ordered from this site.

Angela Adams
Textiles and furniture are new designs imbued with midcentury modern spirit. Purchase from the website, angelaadams.com or call 800/255-9454 to place phone orders or find a local retailer.

Circa50
circa50.com
Vintage modern furniture, lighting, and fabrics.

Dansk Mobel Kunst dmk.dk
Offers vintage Scandinavian furniture from the 1920s to 1975, including original pieces and rare collector's items. Shipping and customs can add up to $650 to the cost of a purchase.

Deco-echoes.com
Online shops, galleries, catalog, and magazine.

Design Within Reach
Modern classics still in production or reintroduced; also, contemporary designs. Call 800/944-2233 for a catalog or to purchase online, visit dwr.com

Gomod.com
A portal to online shops, store locator by region and zipcode, bulletin boards, and more.

Hi+Lo Modern
hiandlomodern.com
Twentieth-century artifacts, including glass, furniture, lighting, and photography.

Industrial Home
European decorative arts and design from the 20th century. Call 212/260-3132 for information or visit industrial-home.com

Jetset
jetsetmodern.com
Vintage furniture, decorative arts, lighting, electronics, and more.

Mid-Century Seating
midcenturyseating.com
Classic midcentury designs manufactured by Herman Miller, Knoll, Thonet, and others into the 1980s.

ModHaus
modhaus.com
Online gallery of vintage furnishings and decorative arts from the 1950s to 1970s, with an emphasis on American and Scandinavian.

Room&Board
Call 800/486-6554 for a catalog or shop online
roomandboard.com
New furnishings and lighting inspired by traditional and modern classics.

Simply Mod
simplymod.com
Modern design objects, including furniture, lighting, and electronics, from 1950s-1970s.

Sonrisa
sonrisafurniture.com
Reclaimed and restored metal furniture and objects from America's "Steel Age"; also new metal furniture designs.

TwentiethCenturyDesigns.com
Click on "Links" to find lists of vintage modern shops and sites worth visiting.

Unicahome.com
Contemporary furnishings and accessories with a modern/retro spirit, plus contemporary Italian design

Vintage Express
vintageexpress.com
A site that leads to auctions and online malls and offers free Classifed pages for buying and selling vintage modern pieces.

Vintage Modern Design
vintagemoderndesign.com
Specializes in 1950s–1970s

design objects—including furniture, housewares, and lighting.

Worth a Visit

Northeast

Abodeon
1731 Massachusetts Ave., Cambridge, MA. 617/497-0137. Vintage modern furnishings and accessories, and new industrial design. Call for shop hours and directions.

American Decorative Arts
3 Olive St.
Northampton, MA.
800-3-MODERN
decorativearts.com
This company is the parent of three subsidiary companies: Chris Kennedy Antiques deals exclusively in modern furnishings attributable to a known designer or manufacturer; Schmieg & Kotzian, a custom furniture company that will reproduce early modern classics to order, using original specifications; and Designbase, a library of primary sources and information on modern architecture and design.

The Conran Shop
Located under the 59th Street Bridge in New York City, The Conran Shop offers a distinctive mix of contemporary, classic modern,

and global design; furniture, accessories, lighting, textiles, bedding, dinnerware, and giftware. To shop online, visit www.conran.com

Donzella
17 White St.
New York, NY. 212/965-8919
donzella.com
Extensive collection of vintage modern furniture and significant designs, furniture, and decorative pieces from California estates. Also American and European furniture, lighting, and decorative arts from 1920-1960.

IKEA
Synonymous with modern, functional design at affordable prices, IKEA also offers simple classic pieces. Unfortunately, no online store; visit Ikea-usa.com for store locations and to browse the virtual catalog.

Lost City Arts
18 Cooper Sq.
New York, NY. 212/375-0500
lostcityarts.com
Features original 20th-century design and architectural objects, as well as reproduction furniture, lighting, and design accessories

Museum of Modern Art Design Store
81 Spring St., New York, NY
646/613-1367
44 West 53rd St., New York, NY
212/767-1050
Original contemporary products for office and home: desk accessories, tabletop,

travel accessories, furniture, lighting, toys. For more information or to shop online, visit MoMa.org

Nuovo Melodrom
60 Green Street, New York, NY
212/219-0013. New modern classics and contemporary Italian design; call to order a catalog or shop online at nuovomelodrom.com

R 20th Century Design
82 Franklin Street
New York, NY
212/343-7979; r20thcentury.com
Visit the showroom or the website to survey an international selection of unique and well-crafted objects, lighting, and furniture from the midcentury modern movement. The website also includes excellent biographies of modern architects and designers.

Regeneration Modern Furniture
38 Renwick St.
New York, NY. 212/741-2102
www.regenerationfurniture.com
Midcentury modern vintage furniture, with a focus on the 1950s and specializing in vintage pieces from American and Danish designers.

White Furniture
85 White Street
New York, NY. 212/964-4694
whiteonwhite.com
Modern icons at affordable prices.

Southeast

FUTURES Antiques
3824 Granby Street
Norfolk, VA. 757/624-2050
email: futures@exis.net
Visit on the web:
deco-echoes.com/futures

Galere
3733 South Dixie Highway
West Palm Beach, FL
561/832-3611; galere.net
Features 20th-century furniture,
glass, lighting.

Good Eye
4918 Wisconsin Avenue NW
Washington, DC. 202/244-8516
goodeyeonline.com
Furniture and accessories from
1950s-1970s.

Highbrow Inc.
2110 8th Ave. South, Nashville,
TN. Modern classics still in
production, including Herman
Miller; visit the store or shop
online at highbrowfurniture.com

Hollis & Knight Ltd.
3320 M St. NW, Washington,
D.C. 202/333-6999
Offers a sophisticated mix of
traditional furniture, Italian
modern, and antiques.

Modernism Gallery
1622 Ponce de Leon Blvd.
Coral Gables, FL
305/442-8743; modernism.com
Original Art Deco and
American modernist furniture,
lighting, and accessories.

Retro Modern
805 Peachtree Street
Atlanta, GA. 404/724-0093;
retromodern.com
Midcentury modern and late
1960s to the present.

Senzatempo
1655 Meridian Ave.
Miami Beach, FL
305/534-5588; senzatempo.com
Specializes in designer
furniture and decorative arts
from 1930-1960.

Midwest

AOkay Antiques
124-5th St., West Des Moines,
IA. 515/255-2525; Victorian to
modern, with an emphasis on
1950s collectibles.

Christines
309 E. 5th St., Des Moines, IA.
515/243-3500. Vintage modern
furniture and accessories.

Design Ranch Store & Studio
701 East Davenport St., Iowa
City, IA. 800/311-4696
designranch@aol.com

DesignSmith Gallery
1342 Main Street
Cincinnati, Ohio. 513/421-1397
designsmithgallery.com
Focuses on vintage furnishings
from the Art Deco, midcentury
modern, and 1960s-1970s
movements.

IKEA
Visit ikea-usa.com for Chicago
store location and to browse
the virtual catalog.

No Place Like
300 W. Grand Ave.
Chicago, IL. 312/822-0550
Contemporary furnishings and
accessories
noplacelike.net (or email:
info@noplacelike.net)

Pavilion
pavilionantiques.com
2055 North Damen, Chicago,
IL. 773/645-0924. Specializing in
19th-century and mid-20th-
century French design, Italian,
Scandinavian, and industrial
design.

**Projects: A Contemporary
Showroom**
501 E. Locust St., Des Moines,
IA. 515/557-1833. Contemporary
furniture and design classics
still in production.

Retro Inferno
1712 Main St., Kansas City, MO
816/842-4004

Springdale Furnishings
19 South Elm Street, Three
Oaks, Michigan. 269/756-9896.
Summer: daily 11 a.m–6 p.m.
Winter: Fri.–Mon. 11 a.m.–6 p.m.,
Tues.–Thurs. by appointment.
Heywood-Wakefield furniture,
vintage and restored; also
midcentury modern
accessories, lighting, and more.
springdalefurnishings.com

Succotash
781 Raymond Ave., St. Paul, MN
651/603-8787

Southwest

Century Modern
2928 Main St.
Dallas, TX. 214/651-9200
www.centurymodern.com
Vintage furniture, lighting, and
microphones from 1940s-1970.

Collage 20th Century Classics
1300 North Industrial Blvd.,
Dallas, TX. 214/828-9888.
collageclassics.com Features
furniture, decorative arts, and
lighting. Call to order.

Do Wah Diddy
3642 E. Thomas Rd.
Phoenix, AZ. dowahdiddy.com
New and vintage retro items.

Eurway
Three store locations (Dallas,
Austin, and Houston) and an
online shopping site offering
international contemporary
design at low, direct-import
prices. eurway.com

Modern Furniture OKC
8913 North Western Ave
Oklahoma City, OK

modernfurnitureokc.com
Furniture, lighting, accessories, and textiles from 1950s-1970s.

West

Carla
7466 Beverly Blvd. Ste. 101
Los Angeles, CA. 323/932-6064
carlainc.com. Modern furniture and objects from 1940s-1970s. Items are pictured on the website and may be purchased by phone.

Decodence
1684 Market St.
San Francisco, CA. 415/553-4525; decodence.com
Online store features a sample of the many items available in the showroom.

IKEA
Visit ikea-usa.com for store locations and to browse the virtual catalog.

Modern One
7958 Beverly Blvd., Los Angeles, CA. Visit online at artofcollecting.net

Sam Kaufman
7965 Beverly Blvd., Los Angeles, CA. 323/857-1965. artofcollecting.net

Vintage Modern
182 Gough St.
San Francisco, CA. 415/861-8162
Vintage home furnishings and lighting.

Wazee Deco
383 Corona Street
Denver, CO. 303/293-2144; wazeedeco.com
Visit the store or shop online; the store maintains an inventory of over 3,000 museum-quality midcentury pieces, Art Deco, Art Nouveau, and 1950s furniture.

Credits

Pages 10-21
Interior design: Leo Mark
Hampton Interiors, ASID
1100 Ayshire St., Orlando, FL 32803
407/897-5288
Wall color: Sherwin Williams Dove Grey
Page 13: chair seat fabric, Gretchen Belenger

Page 14: Draperies Scalamandré, blinds by Conrad. Flokati rug: ABC Carpet and Home.

Page 16: Platner stool (and armchairs) available from Knoll; for a local dealer, check "locations" on knoll.com. Platner collection available online with choice of upholstery fabrics from highbrowfurniture.com; Barcelona table also available from highbrowfurniture.com.

Page 17: Akari lamp by Isamu Noguchi. Table Model UF2-31N. Visit the Isamu Noguchi Garden Museum Store online to purchase: store.yahoo.com/akaristore

Page 19: Saarinen dining table available from Knoll. Visit knoll.com to find local dealers.

Pages 22-35
Interior design: Benjamin Noriega-Ortiz
Benjamin Noriega-Ortiz, LLC
75 Spring Street, 6th Floor
New York, NY 10012
212/343-9709
bnodesign.com
Pages 26–27: Aluminum stacked table, reissue of 1932 table; Lost City (see Resources). Womb chair and ottoman, designed by Eero Saarinen. Knoll continues to manufacture these chairs; to find a local dealer, visit knoll.com. Reproductions are offered by highbrowfurniture.com. Ero/S/Chair (clear polycarbonate pedestal chair) by Philippe Starck, available from Design Within Reach, dwr.com.

Page 30: Noguchi table lamp Model 1N Akari Light Sculptures available from store.yahoo.com/akaristore

Page 32: Encaustic landscape by Hiro Yokose from Stephen Haller Gallery, New York, New York.

Page 33: Feathered lamp: custom design from And Bob's Your Uncle; for information, visit

the website www.andbobsyouruncle.com

Pages 36-51
FUTURES Antiques
3824 Granby Street
Norfolk, VA 23504
757/624-2050
email: futures@exis.net
Visit on the web: www.deco-echoes.com/futures
Store hours: Wed. 12-7 p.m. Thurs.-Sun. 12-5 p.m.
For inventory advance update lists (by email), send a request by email.
Ronn's Noguchi coffee table is vintage, but you can buy a new one through Design Within Reach, dwr.com; 800/944-2233; also Room & Board; call 800/486-6554 for a catalog or shop online roomandboard.com.

Pages 54-61
Interior design: Beth Sachse
SR Hughes Showroom
1345 East 15th St.
Tulsa, OK 74120
918/582-4999
SR Hughes Showroom is an exclusive retail and to-the-trade resource featuring custom designs, original artwork, selected antiques and primitives, Flos lighting, Odegard Tibetan rugs, and Italian classic modern furnishings from Cassina and Giorgetti.
Landscape design: Kelly Dixon
1509 E. 11th St.
Tulsa, OK 74120
918/599-7707
gardenenvironments.com
Grand Confort chair designed by Le Corbusier, Charlotte Perriand, and Pierre Jeanneret; produced by Cassina to original design specifications. Dining table and "Cab" dining chairs also by Cassina. To find a dealer near

you, call 800/770-3568 or visit online cassinausa.com

Pages 62-71
Red chair and ottoman, side table, pillows on chair, white lamp, gold chair, coffee table, buffet, dining table: Dialogica, 484 Broome St., New York, NY 10013; 212/966-1934; for information and store locations, visit the website at DialogicaDesign.com.
Page 64: red lamp, Roche-Bobois USA Ltd. For store locations write 183 Madison Ave., New York, NY 10016. Sofa fabric, curtains: Donghia. Armoire: Z Gallerie; for store locations, call 310/527-6811 or visit online zgallerie.com

Pages 66-67: shelf on dining room wall: Palazzetti; 212/832-1199. Pedestal dish, vase with stars, decanter and glasses, plate: Kosta Boda, through Orrefors Crystal Group, Inc., Berlin, NJ; 609/768-5400. Pitcher and glasses on table: Pier 1. Painting: Eric Zener, available through Hespe Gallery hespe.com

Page 68: kitchen table and chairs: California Design Center, Tucson, AZ; 520/881-3700.

Pages 72-83
Architect: William A. Schulz
8 Main St.
Southampton, NY 11968
631/287-4216
Page 74: Heywood-Wakefield Lazy Susan cocktail table available from Heywood-Wakefield, 2300 SW 23rd St.,

Miami, FL 33145; 305/858-4240; heywoodwakefield.com. The original company closed its doors in the 1970s; the new firm makes new and retro pieces; no vintage pieces are available.

Page 76: Aalto high stool available new from Herman Miller; to find a retailer near you or an online retail source, visit online hermanmiller.com

Pages 78-79: dining chairs similar to those shown but with honey-toned finish available from Heywood-Wakefield; see above.

Pages 84-93 Contractor/builder: Jeff Fairey, Vintage Contemporary, Dallas, Texas; 214/824-2579.
Paints: living areas, Martha Stewart H22 Vellum; kitchen, Martha Stewart G23 Winter Surf.
Pages 86-87: Sofas: Eames Sofa Compact; purchased through Collage, a vintage modern retail store in Dallas; 214/828-9888. Available new through Herman Miller; to find a retailer near you or an online retail source, visit hermanmiller.com or hmhome.com
Pillows: Jonathan Adler, purchased from Smink, Dallas, 214/350-0542. For store locations, visit online jonathanadler.com

Pages 88-89: Dining chairs: Emeco naval side chairs available from Design Within Reach, dwr.com. Buffet: B&B Italia, from Smink. For B&B Italia store locations visit bebitalia.it online, or check with a local interior designer to order.

Pages 92-93: Eames Softback Lounger, Isamu Noguchi coffee table, Eames Plywood Lounge Chair available from Design Within Reach, dwr.com. Coffee table and molded plywood lounge chair also available from Room & Board; call 800/486-6554 for a catalog or visit online roomandboard.com. Floor lamp, Oriac Design, oriacdesign.com. Art in stairwell: by David Bates, available through Dunn & Brown Contemporary Art Gallery, 214/521-4322.

Pages 94-109
To order a catalog or purchase Angela Adams textiles and furniture by Sherwood Hamill, visit online at angelaadams.com

Pages 110-117
Ross Levy
Levy Art & Architecture Inc.
3361 Mission St.
San Francisco, CA 94110
415/641-7320
Visit online at 10d.com
Pages 112-113: coffee table, IKEA (owner had glass top sandblasted). Bertoia lounge chair available new from Knoll; visit knoll.com and check "locations" for a dealer near you. Sofa from Fruewirth Design, San Diego.

Pages 118-133
Architect: Laney Vickers, AIA
The Architects' Office
1712 Rio Grande, Suite F
Austin, TX 78707
512/478-5555
Interior design: Kris Walsh, 972/479-1030; and Dan and Kimberly Renner
Kolbe & Kolbe windows throughout: Grand Openings

512/989-9400
Pages 120-121: Gangchen Snow Leopard rug, David Alan Rugs, 512/499-0456. Paint: Sherwin-Williams 1102, walls; 1101, trim.

Page 122: Tibetan Blocks rug by Barbara Barry, Tufenkian Designers Reserve, 800/582-0569; and David Alan Rugs, see above. Fire screen: Two Hills Studio, 512/707-7575. Pastel by Will K!em: Wally Workman, 512/472-7428. Wall and trim paint: Sherwin-Williams 1101. Knoll love seat: available new from Knoll; visit knoll.com to find a dealer in your area.

Pages 124-125: kitchen cabinetry: Homestead Heritage, 254/829-2060. Wall paint Sherwin Williams 1102; trim, Sherwin Williams 1101. Chandelier in breakfast area: Gardens, 512/451-5490. Stuffed chair in family room: Expressions Custom Furniture; 800/544-4519.

Pages 126-127: Bed linens and netting: The Homestead, 830/997-5551. Wall paint: Benjamin Moore 1018; trim Sherwin-Williams 1059.

Pages 132-133: Indonesian chest and lamp, Gardens; 512/451-5490.

Pages 136-151
No Place Like
300 W. Grand Ave.
Chicago, IL 60610
312/822-0550
noplacelike.net (or email: info@noplacelike.net)

Pages 136-137: Cube Chair and Tube Floor Lamp by In House, available through No Place Like. Hand-cast acrylic table designed by Robert Kirkbride, through No Place Like.

Pages 138-139: "Circle 3" end table by In House, through No Place Like.

Pages 140-141: Block-printed silk wall hanging: Kermit Berg, 773/583-9613. Sofas by Carter. Mosaic table: Crate and Barrel.

Pages 142-143: Black vase to left of fireplace: Jonathan Adler, through No Place Like, or check for retail sources near you by visiting online jonathanadler.com. White birch lamp with veneer shade: by dform, available through No Place Like. Blue glass vase also through No Place Like.

Pages 144-145: Vases by Eva Zeisel for KleinReed, available through No Place Like.

Pages 146-147: Buffet, Room & Board; call 800/486-6554 for a catalog, or visit online roomandboard.com. Eames chairs from Herman Miller (visit hermanmiller.com to find a local retailer), or order online at eameschairsandmore.com. Table base: IKEA. Fused glass platter by Kathleen Ash, Studio K, Austin, Texas, through No Place Like. Bud vases, No Place Like.

Pages 150-151: bedding by

Archipelago; suede pillows by Golden Bear; chrome cylinder lamp by Biproduct. Aorta vase by Jonathan Adler. Digital montages by Kermit Berg. All available through No Place Like.

Pages 152-161
Design: Liz Zamadics
Pages 154-155: black and white photographs, Stephen Zamadics Photography, 512/918-8306; zamadics.com. Coffee tables: Lack triangular side tables, IKEA, 800/434-4532. Floor lamps, Alang, IKEA. Wall paint: Ralph Lauren Paints, Ghurka; 800/379-7656.

Pages 156-157: stainless steel tray on ottoman: Groggy, IKEA, 800/434-4532; ikea-usa.com. Martini glasses, Optimal, IKEA. Lamp in sunroom: Galar, IKEA. Martini pitcher and bud vase on tray, Pottery Barn, 800/922-5507; potterybarn.com. Leopard ottoman, Custom Creations And, 1500 West Alabama, Houston, TX; 713/522-5833. Silverleaf glass-topped table, Area, 5600 Kirby Dr., Houston, TX; 713/668-1668. Black/tan arc silk pillows: Cities, 1905 Westheimer, Houston, TX; 713/528-2662. Camel linen throw pillows, Pottery Barn.

Page 158: dining table Granas, IKEA; 800/434-4532. Black lamps on sideboard: Kuhl-Linscomb, 2424 West Alabama, Houston, TX; 713/526-6000. Glass bud vases, Pottery Barn, 800/922-5507; potterybarn.com. Wall paint: Ralph Lauren Paints Ghurka; call 800/379-7656 for nearest dealer or color help.

Pages 160-161: pencil post bed: Ethan Allen; 800/228-9229; ethanallen.com. Bedside table lamps Husa, IKEA. Beaded linen throw pillows, Pottery Barn.

Pages 162-173
Greg Mewbourne Designs
1903-A Oxmoor Road
Birmingham, AL 35209
205/871-6438
Page 163: Sculpture on hearth, Darren Hardman, Birmingham, Alabama; available through Monty Stabler Galleries, 205/879-9888. Crown-shape crystal bowl on server by William Yeoward; check williamyeowardcrystal.com for a dealer in your area.

Page 164-165: Mies van der Rohe M544 chairs produced by Knoll as MR Armchair. Lamp in front of window: Maguire. Tray coffee table: Baker.

Pages 168-169: kitchen stools by Granger Carr, AD Antiquity, Birmingham, AL. Chairs in dining room: Maui stacking side chair, Design Within Reach, dwr.com

Pages 170-171: headboard upholstery, vinyl from Glantt Fabrics, Modern Collection: Liquid Leather. Shell lamp: Hoosin Lampworks; hoosin.com. Painting by David Kidd; for information visit jackmeiergallery.com.

Pages 174-183
Clifford M. Welch, AIA
Dallas, Texas
214/327-3707

Pages 176-177: sofa, B&B Italia, from Smink, Dallas. For retailers near you who offer B&B Italia products, visit the website bebitalia.it. Chairs: Alvar Aalto Pension Chair, available online at aalto.com. Platform Bench by George Nelson, from Herman Miller; available through Design Within Reach, dwr.com. Floor lamp: Isamu Noguchi, from Design Within Reach or from the Isamu Noguchi Garden Museum Store, store.yahoo.com/akaristore.

Page 179: new Cesca side chairs manufactured according to original specifications available through Palazzetti

Pages 180-181: dresser, B&B Italia. Dresser lamps, Elise, Design Within Reach. Eames Lounge Chair, Design Within Reach.

Page 182: Chaises, PT Skate Collection by Paul Tuttle, from Vecta.

Page 200: Photos of Florence Knoll, Mies van der Rohe, and Isamu Noguchi courtesy of Knoll. Photos of George Nelson and Charles Eames courtesy of Herman Miller.

INDEX